TULIPS

TULIPS

beautiful varieties for home and garden

JANE EASTOE

photography by

RACHEL WARNE

GIBBS SMITH
TO ENRICH AND INSPIRE HUMANKIND

Contents

INTRODUCTION

IN THE DINING ROOM OF MY CHILDHOOD HOME THERE HUNG A STILL-LIFE PAINTING OF A BANQUETING SCENE. IT SHOWED A RUMPLED TABLECLOTH ON WHICH FRUIT WAS PILED UP, SOME CUT OPEN. A DEAD PHEASANT LAY WAITING FOR PLUCKING, THERE WAS A CONGENIAL HALF-EMPTY GLASS OF WINE, AND A VAST FLOWER ARRANGEMENT DROPPED WITHERED PETALS ON TO THE CLOTH BELOW. I WAS MESMERIZED BY THIS OTHER WORLD SO VERY DIFFERENT FROM OUR OWN, BUT IT WAS THE FIERY BEAUTY OF THE STRIPED AND FEATHERED BLOOMS THAT REALLY CAPTURED MY HEART.

I did not recognize them as the same flowers that dominated the spring bedding schemes of the meticulously groomed local municipal gardens. Here, true to my town's Victorian heritage, ranks of crimson and yellow tulips stood to attention, gaudy primulas at their feet. This bilious display did not show the flowers to their best advantage and it was not until 20 years later, on a visit to Christopher Lloyd's garden at Great Dixter in East Sussex, that I finally understood the allure of tulips and identified the exquisite painted blooms of my youth.

The flamboyant cultivated tulips we love have been bred from species tulips, the wild forms which grow naturally in the mountainous regions of Russia, Kazakhstan, Uzbekistan, Mongolia and China. Long centuries ago – precisely when, nobody knows – the natives of the region recognized that the plants had some value and dug up the bulbs for trading. Thus the tulip began its creep westwards, via the Silk Road. Gradually their reach extended and their fame spread. By the 16th century tulips had reached the heart of the Ottoman Empire in Turkey and were celebrated in Ottoman culture.

Species tulips are petite things, possessed of a rare and quiet beauty but also some flamboyant coloration. What most have in common is the knack for variation, and the regular production of sports in their progeny. This trait has led to considerable confusion for botanists, who still debate whether certain species are true or mere variants of another. Yet this same trait for infinite variation delighted Ottoman gardeners, who quickly exploited it in the cultivation of new, showier forms. So prevalent was the tulip in Turkey on high days and holidays that the English poet George Sandys (1578–1644) observed in his book *A relation of a journey begun An: Dom: 1610*: "You cannot stirre abroad, but you shall be presented by the Dervishes and Janizaries with tulips and trifles."

The popularity of this flower, as yet unknown in Europe, resulted in it being mentioned in dispatches by ambassadors to the Ottoman Empire, who shipped bulbs home. The first recorded sighting of a tulip in Europe was in 1559, in a garden in Augsburg, then part of the Holy Roman Empire, now Germany. The first officially accepted date of a tulip blooming in the Netherlands is 1594 and it quickly became a status symbol, creating a market that is still vital to the Dutch economy today.

The business of bulb cultivation

Trading in tulips was initially relatively easy. Species tulips produce seed that is true to type, and it takes three years to develop a bulb from seed that is sufficiently mature to produce a flower. Species tulips also reproduce vegetatively, sending out stoloniferous growths that go deeper into the soil and produce new, immature bulbs.

Cultivated tulips are quite another matter. The process of breeding new cultivars is slow, and seed from cultivated tulips does not grow true to type. Therefore, cultivars are propagated via bulb offsets – genetic clones – which are produced by the mother tulip. A tulip is usually ready to be lifted six to eight weeks after flowering and the soil is brushed away from the bulb so that the offsets are visible. These can then be gently twisted away from the mother bulb, checked over, and stored in a cool, dry place to rest over the summer, replicating the conditions of their natural habitat. Larger offsets may bloom the following year, while small offsets need to be grown for two to three years in nursery beds until ready to bloom. The cultivated mother bulb does not repeat flower as a rule and can be discarded when the offsets are removed.

From hundreds of experimental cross-bred plants, only one may have commercial potential. It takes 20 years for a breeder to bring a new cultivar to market, and stock in any one year is finite. Aside from the financial lure of uncovering a new cultivar of spectacular beauty, tulip breeders have to continue in their endeavors because most modern cultivars do not have an indefinite lifespan, even when reproduced by offsets. After a while the clones gradually become less vigorous, the bulb stocks diminish and eventually the cultivar disappears.

Nature can also throw in a curveball, for cultivars are capable of mutating. A breeder strolling through fields of a single variety may come across a sport which is quite different from the parent flower in color or form. They will then assess whether this fluke of nature has commercial potential in its own right.

The lifespan of a new cultivar, or sport, cannot be predicted; some survive for only 30 years. Some survive year in year out, but these are few and far between and it is not yet known why their clones do not age, while others do. It is for this reason that the tulip market evolves constantly, and we should not be too precious about purchasing a new cultivar because an old favorite is unobtainable.

Tulip fanciers place their bulb orders early in the buying season (late summer to late autumn), even though tulip bulbs should not be planted out until late autumn. Early ordering ensures devotees can lay their hands on the most desirable cultivars and it is quite common to find that hot new cultivars are sold out when the buying season has only just gotten under way.

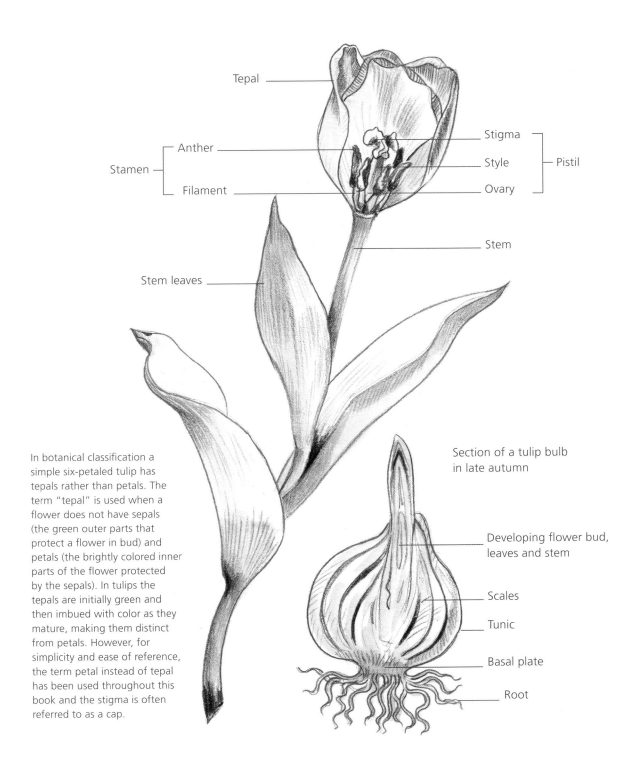

Tepal

Stamen
Anther
Filament

Stigma
Style
Ovary
Pistil

Stem

Stem leaves

Section of a tulip bulb
in late autumn

In botanical classification a simple six-petaled tulip has tepals rather than petals. The term "tepal" is used when a flower does not have sepals (the green outer parts that protect a flower in bud) and petals (the brightly colored inner parts of the flower protected by the sepals). In tulips the tepals are initially green and then imbued with color as they mature, making them distinct from petals. However, for simplicity and ease of reference, the term petal instead of tepal has been used throughout this book and the stigma is often referred to as a cap.

Developing flower bud,
leaves and stem

Scales

Tunic

Basal plate

Root

Selection

Tulips are cultivated in numerous forms, defined either by group or by numerical divisions. The Royal General Bulb Growers' Association (KAVB) serves as the international cultivar registration authority for bulbs, including tulips, as well as corms and tubers. Before any new cultivar is registered, breeders and growers will first cultivate it in test beds to see how it performs, then build up stock before its introduction.

The groups listed below define the characteristics of different types of tulip and help to clarify the type of bloom, habit and time of flowering. If you familiarize yourself with the groups you will find it easier to purchase a selection of cultivars to suit your individual requirements and help you to have a good show of tulips from early to late spring.

SINGLE EARLY (Division One)
Flowering from early spring to mid-spring, tulips in this class produce a single, six-petaled flower head per stalk.
Height: 8–14in (20–35cm)

DOUBLE EARLY (Division Two)
These tulips produce flower heads with double sets of petals, borne on short, strong stems from early spring to mid-spring.
Height: 8–12in (20–30cm)

TRIUMPH (Division Three)
The hybridization of Single Early tulips and Darwin tulips created a class that produces blooms with an angular cupped shape in a broad array of colors, flowering in mid-spring.
Height: 10–16in (25–40cm)

DARWIN HYBRIDS (Division Four)
Created from the hybridization of Darwin tulips, species tulips and cultivated tulips, Darwin Hybrids produce big blooms in a glorious array of intense colors within the red, yellow, orange and pink spectrum; the petals may be blotched and striped. The plants flower in mid-spring.
Height: 12–20in (30–50cm)

SINGLE LATE (Division Five)
This class often features in bedding displays as it produces some of the tallest tulips. Brightly colored flowers bloom from mid-spring to late spring and are carried on tall stems.
Height: 10–30in (25–75cm)

LILY-FLOWERED (Division Six)
This class produces distinctively shaped blooms with pointed rather than rounded petals. The plants bloom in mid-spring.
Height: 14–30in (35–75cm)

FRINGED (Division Seven)
This class is easily recognized by the fringes that decorate the tips of each petal. The bulbs were cultivated from mutants of Single Early tulips and the plants flower in late spring.
Height: 8–30in (20–75cm)

VIRIDIFLORA (Division Eight)

The blooms of this class of tulips resemble those of the Lily-flowered group in shape but are easily distinguished by the stripe of green that runs from the base to the tip of each petal. The plants bloom in late spring.
Height: 12–24in (30–60cm)

REMBRANDT (Division Nine)

These are the exquisite blooms with striped and streaked petals that were immortalized by the Dutch Old Masters. As the distinctive patterning was caused by a virus which is deadly to many other plants, these particular tulips are no longer available from bulb suppliers, although a few private collectors still cultivate them. Fortunately, growers have developed cultivars with similar markings that can be sold commercially.

PARROT (Division Ten)

These showy extroverts of the tulip family have curled, waved and pleated petals in a fabulous array of colors. Descended from mutations from the Single Late and Triumph classes, these plants bloom from mid-spring to late spring.
Height: 12–20in (30–50cm)

DOUBLE LATE (Division Eleven)

Sometimes dubbed peony tulips, these multi-petaled beauties produce double flowers that can reach an impressive 8in (20cm) in diameter when fully open. They are carried on strong stems in late spring.
Height: 12–16in (30–40cm)

KAUFMANNIANA (Division Twelve)

Cultivated from the species *Tulipa kaufmanniana*, a native of Central Asia, this early-blooming class produces flowers with pointed petals that open into flattened star shapes. They bloom in early spring.
Height: 4–8in (10–20cm)

FOSTERIANA (Division Thirteen)

Cultivated from the species *Tulipa fosteriana*, which hails from the mountains of Central Asia, this class produces distinctive blooms with blunt-edged petals, each with a small point at the tip. Some cultivars have foliage with stripes or mottled patterns. The plants bloom from early spring to mid-spring.
Height: 8–20in (20–50cm)

GREIGII (Division Fourteen)

Cultivated from the species *Tulipa greigii*, another native of Central Asia, this class is known for its brilliant coloration and distinctive foliage, the leaves often being patterned with stripes, dashes and mottling. The plant flowers from early spring to mid-spring.
Height: 8–12in (20–30cm)

SPECIES (Division Fifteen)

These are the original botanical species that grow naturally in the wild, the parents of all cultivated forms. Most species tulips are shorter and have smaller flower heads. In theory they will naturalize if left *in situ*, but some species require a very particular set of growing conditions, notably good drainage and dry conditions in summer. If you plant them in pots it is easier to replicate their natural habitat and shelter them from the rain in summer.

MISCELLANEOUS

Occasionally a new cultivar does not fit neatly into any of the above categories and is classed as Miscellaneous.

The work of hybridizers across these groups has resulted in the production of some of the most beautiful flowers in the world. The flames once created by the dreaded mosaic virus (the only known instance of a virus improving the look of a plant, although inevitably weakening it too) have now been bred into new cultivars; sculpted parrot tulips stand proud and tall; towering Darwins light up the flower bed and even repeat flower for a year or two; Lily-flowered tulips have the most elegant of forms, and peony-like cultivars with their great petticoat blooms cannot fail to delight.

This book is designed to be an inspirational introduction to growing your own tulips. There are thousands of cultivars to choose from, with more being released every year. Here I present a selection of personal favorites, a mix of established cultivars and the new releases. As these stunning pictures by photographer Rachel Warne illustrate, there are tulip cultivars to suit every taste and every garden color scheme. Not every tulip photographed has a full profile, but if it has struck your fancy seek it out. Garden centers tend to offer just a few limited varieties, if you want a particular specimen a specialist tulip nursery will be able to help you – they are easy enough to find on the internet. Do think about shopping for tulips in the summer as the most popular cultivars can sell out by early autumn.

There are four themed chapters to highlight the incredible range on offer; in The Classic Bloom you'll find tulips with perfect shape and form celebrated in a range of colors, from soft neutrals and pastels to dramatic reds and purples. The Opulent Flower chapter salutes the richest colored tulips, some with bold, contrasting stripes and whorls designed to make the garden vibrate with color. We pay homage to the exotic blooms that sparked tulip fever in the chapter The Mosaic Beauty; here you will find blooms shot through with myriad hues and decorated with flames and feathering. In The Whimsical Delight we celebrate the tulip's dramatic range of form and unusual coloration. Be seduced by shy species tulips, cultivars that have waisted or starry flowers, and blooms with fringed or twisted petals.

That the tulip is a fabulous flower is indisputable. However, some people complain that unlike daffodils they do not repeat flower for successive years. The problem is not with the tulip, but with our expectation of it. Although species tulips will repeat flower if planted in exactly the right conditions, cultivated tulips mostly do not unless they are lifted and the offsets are given the correct storage over the summer. Do this and you will ensure that you have tulips in your garden year in, year out. Adding new varieties to your stock every so often is sensible because few cultivars will reproduce via offsets indefinitely.

The task is not onerous, and the payback is immeasurable. People once had to shell out a small fortune for the privilege of growing a tulip; we can now all afford to plant at least a few bulbs. What better way to herald the arrival of spring?

THE HISTORY OF TULIPS

IN 1735, THE SWEDISH BOTANIST, PHYSICIAN AND ZOOLOGIST CARL LINNAEUS INTRODUCED A FORMAL SYSTEM OF BINOMIAL NOMENCLATURE WHICH WAS DESIGNED TO GIVE ALL LIVING THINGS A UNIQUE SCIENTIFIC CLASSIFICATION. PLANTS HAD BEEN DESCRIBED AND CATALOGUED PREVIOUSLY, BUT THIS UNIVERSAL SYSTEM WOULD ENSURE A CONSISTENT REFERENCE.

However, unlike many other plants known to Linnaeus, tulips were something of a mystery. There were no ancient references to the tulip in Europe. No observations from Greek or Roman botanists in their travels; no records of tulips in medieval herbals; indeed, no hint of their existence until the 16th century.

To some degree this lack of information can be explained by the fact that many species tulips – the genetic forebears of our modern cultivars – hail from the East, growing wild in the remote mountain regions of Tien Shan and Pamir-Alai in what is now Tajikistan, Uzbekistan, Kyrgyzstan, Kazakhstan, Turkestan and China. Other species have been observed growing in the Caucasus on the borders of Western Asia and Eastern Europe, and in Iran, Turkey, Algeria, Morocco, Italy, Greece and Crete.

There are currently more than 300 recorded species tulips. Many were gathered in the 18th and 19th centuries by enthusiastic plant-hunters who believed they had uncovered new species in their original habitats, but the true origins of the more westerly species are now unclear. Contemporary scientific research using DNA sequencing suggests that the real number of tulip species stands at just 76 in total, the rest being naturalized imports, mere variants of their eastern parents.

The travels of the tulip

The tulip's journey west began with traders along the Silk Road, a network of trade routes from east to west established during China's Han Dynasty (206BCE–220CE). Initially devoted to the transportation of silk, as you might expect from the name, the trade expanded in range. When it was realized that wild tulip bulbs were of value they too entered the trade route, transported to markets such as those in Samarkand and Tashkent in Uzbekistan and onwards from there.

By the 12th century the tulip had become a popular motif on ceramic tiles that decorated mosques and palaces across the vast empire of the Seljuk Turks, which spread across great swathes of Asia and west into Anatolia, now Turkey. Later, the flower was adopted as a motif by the Ottoman Turks and was emblazoned on manuscripts, textiles, tiles, gravestones and even armor. Both Mughal and Ottoman rulers created gardens filled with tulips, some from species collected in the course of expanding their respective empires, and the tulip became the symbol of the Ottoman dynasty.

Over the centuries the Turks had become experienced in the business of tulip-breeding, and in the 17th century the tulip-growers of Istanbul formed a council to regulate the quality, pricing and naming of the plant. Needle tulips – single-color, almond-shaped flowers with thin pointed petals – were the most highly prized cultivars, although by the 18th century bi-color tulips had won approval too.

That the Turks valued the tulip, a flower then unknown in the West, became clear to European travelers in the 16th century. The French lawyer and diplomat Philippe Canaye (1551–1610) traveled to Turkey and wrote in 1575 that the Turks "always carry a tulip in their hand or set in their turban." A few years later, in 1581, the flamboyantly named Ogier Ghiselin de Busbecq (1522–92), later credited with introducing tulips to the West, noted their presence in a book of letters. In this he recalled his eight-year tenure at the Ottoman Court, serving as the Holy Roman Emperor's ambassador at the court of Süleyman the Magnificent. References to the "tulipan" were numerous, and de Busbecq detailed a sighting on a journey to Constantinople: "As we passed through this district we everywhere came across quantities of flowers, narcissi, hyacinths, and tulipans, as the Turks call them. We were surprised to find them flowering in mid-winter, scarcely a favorable season … The tulip has little or no scent, but it is admired for its beauty and the variety of its colors." Dutifully he shipped seeds and bulbs home to Europe.

The Turkish word for tulip is *lâle*. Precisely how the plant acquired the name *Tulipa* is not certain, although the common theory is that it is linked to the Turkish word for turban. Whether this is in reference to the flower's shape, or a translation muddle arising from an inquiry as to the name of the flower the Turks wore tucked into their turbans, is unknown. Nor is it known precisely how or when the tulip reached Europe. The Swiss physician and naturalist Conrad Gesner is credited with the first description and drawing in 1559, when he noted a "*Tulipa turcarum*" in his book *Historia Plantarum* after seeing a tulip in Augsburg, Germany. Linnaeus later named this *T. gesneriana* in his honor.

Tulip cultivation in Europe

The French physician and botanist Carolus Clusius (1526–1609) played an important role in the early promotion and development of the cultivated tulip, as well as in its spread across Europe. In 1573 he was invited to establish a botanic garden in Vienna, for the Holy Roman Emperor Maximilian II. The notion that botany was an academic subject worthy of study was a novel one, although physicians had long studied plants in order to understand their medicinal properties; herbalism was one of the oldest sciences.

In Vienna, Clusius met the aforementioned Ogier Ghiselin de Busbecq, who presented him with tulip seeds he had been sent from Constantinople. This was not the botanist's first encounter with tulips; he had earlier reported that they "bring pleasure to our eyes by their charming variety" and had even consumed one to see if it had any value as a foodstuff (in fact most tulip bulbs are inedible and can cause severe allergic reactions). Nevertheless, these tulip seeds, and others he obtained while in Vienna, allowed Clusius to learn more about the plant's propagation and cultivation. This information he shared with a network of contacts across Europe, eagerly corresponding with more than 300 like-minded plantsmen and relating details of

the tulip's progression from seed to bloom (a process that can take up to six or seven years), as well as exchanging rare seeds and bulbs with them. In 1589 he wrote to the German physician and botanist Joachim Camerarius, "No year passes without my handing out to my friends two or three hundred tulip bulbs which have borne a blossom." Thus, information on the cultivation of this novel plant was passed from one plantsman to the other and the tulips' characteristics and variations were described in detail.

In 1592, Clusius was invited to establish a botanic garden at the newly formed Leiden University in southern Holland. He moved there in 1593, bringing with him a large collection of tulip bulbs which bloomed in 1594. The date is significant, for while it is known that tulips bloomed even earlier in Amsterdam, those in Clusius's garden are generally accepted as the first recorded date a tulip flowered in the Netherlands – a momentous occasion indeed. Botanists such as Clusius fueled fashionable interest, and the rarity of the tulip bulbs they cultivated ensured that the plant became a status symbol.

Given that the tulip is such a familiar plant today, it is difficult to appreciate the degree of excitement that these flowers generated at the time. Not only were they rare collectors' items, and thus prized, but their blooms were held in the highest esteem. Flowers such as roses, pinks and narcissi were dismissed as inferior to the incomparable beauty and superb colors of the tulip. The striped, feathered or "broken" tulips, which Clusius' correspondents were reporting in the 1580s, were the most prized.

Clusius abhorred the trade in plants, commenting in 1594: "This pursuit will in the end be cheapened . . . because even merchants, artisans and low-grade laborers are getting involved in it. For they can see that rich men will sometimes hand out much money in order to buy some little plant that is recommended because it is rare, so that they can boast to their friends that they own it." He refused to sell any of his rare and precious bulbs. Perhaps as a consequence he was the victim of three bulb thefts – two in 1596, and another in 1598. Theft was rampant, and plants were stolen from botanic gardens and private gardens routinely. People kept guard dogs in their gardens or armed their servants and charged them with keeping watch over the garden at night.

The realization that bulb production could be a lucrative business meant that numerous nurseries sprang up in the Netherlands in the early 17th century. By the 1630s most Dutch towns had nurseries, and barely 50 years after their initial introduction tulips became the Netherlands' fourth largest export. The Dutch had become the foremost tulip-growing nation, and the province of Holland, where the sandy soil was ideal for bulb-growing, was the center of activity. Fortunes could be made if a grower succeeded in producing a spectacular tulip. Nevertheless, the business of cultivating tulips is a slow one, and supply was not meeting demand. It was this very scarcity that drove trade and escalated the price of bulbs.

The Dutch Republic, the predecessor of the Netherlands, had been formed in 1581 and quickly came to dominate world trade. The Dutch East India Company was founded in 1602 and port cities such as Delft, Haarlem and Amsterdam experienced a massive growth in international commerce. New industries sprang up in the refining of sugar and tobacco, imported from the burgeoning empire. Power and money was in the hands of thrifty merchants rather than being the sole preserve of the landed gentry, and although the merchants generally steered clear of any displays of conspicuous consumption, owning tulips marked them out as wealthy. The bulbs had the added advantage of being regarded as an investment, for the price of them was still rising.

The tulip's swift promotion took place in the Dutch Golden Age, which lasted from around 1580 to 1670. This was a period of prosperity for trade and industry, and the arts and sciences flourished in the wake of such affluence. Artists became increasingly interested in close scrutiny of the natural world through the still-life genre and tulips were a popular choice of subject. The feathered and flamed subjects were favored, further heightening the general brouhaha about the plants. Extraordinary as it may seem, as the price of tulip bulbs rose, commissioning a painting of a tulip could be more cost-effective than purchasing the real thing.

Broken tulips

The prized "broken" specimens were something of a mystery to the Dutch growers, appearing randomly amid massed ranks of a planting of identical tulips. No one could understand what caused these aberrations. Broken tulips did not grow true from seed, but the offsets of the bulbs would grow true, replicating the exotic patterns of their parent. Good looks aside, their very rarity made them more desirable, even though such specimens were known to be less vigorous. Carolus Clusius observed in *Rariorum plantarum historia* (1601): "Any tulip thus changing its original color is usually ruined afterwards and wanted only to delight its master's eyes with this variety of colors before dying, as if to bid him a last farewell."

Growers had observed, however, that moving tulip bulbs to fresh soil resulted in more of these physical mutations. In an effort to cultivate "breaking" plants they tried all manner of tricks: they planted tulips in soil that was fertilized by the addition of pigeon dung, they added plaster from old walls and they even liberally peppered the soil with powdered paint. They also halved bulbs from red and from white flowers and tied the two different-colored halves together in an effort to promote breaking. Yet no such system of cultivation was effective. In 1637 the Dutch priest Jodocus Cats wrote that in the time of the plague yet another sickness had developed, "the sickness of blommen or floristen," but as no one yet knew that the plague was a disease spread by vectors, why would they suspect that the cause of the beautiful feathering could be a sickness that was similarly transmitted?

The cause of tulip breaking was not discovered until much later. The mycologist Dorothy Cayley (1874–1955) undertook research into tulip break at the John Innes Centre in England. During the bulbs' resting stage, she grafted and plugged tissue from broken bulbs into unbroken ones to determine whether the effect could be artificially produced. More than a quarter of the resulting flowers broke within the first year, and it appeared that the degree of breaking was in proportion to the amount of tissue introduced. In 1927 she concluded that color breaking in tulips was caused by a virus, and that aphids were responsible for its introduction and spread, a theory that was confirmed in the 1930s by further research.

The aphid in question is *Myzus persicae*, also known as the green peach aphid or the peach potato aphid. It acts as a vector for the transmission of viruses, including the mosaic virus, and is today a named agricultural pest in the USA and many other countries. It damages crops of the family Brassicaceae, which includes cabbage, and the nightshade family Solanaceae, which encompasses potatoes and pumpkins. It also affects peach trees. These were a feature of many 17th-century gardens and the aphid's nymphs snacked on tulips' juicy herbaceous growth, thus introducing the virus. Tulip break is the

only known instance of a virus increasing the value of an infected plant.

Tulipa 'Semper Augustus,' a white tulip with crimson flames that was grown from seed in France and sold in 1614, was regarded as the supreme bloom, although we now know that its distinctive patterning was caused by the mosaic virus. According to the Dutch chronicler Nicolaes van Wassenaer, there were only 12 'Semper Augustus' bulbs in existence in 1624 – all, he maintained, in the hands of just one man. A single bulb sold for 1,200 guilders in 1624, at a time when the average annual wage was just 150 guilders. When the market

hit its peak in 1636–7, the speculators' quoted price was 10,000 guilders (over $127,000 today) for a single bulb – although whether there were any to be had was another matter altogether.

Tulip fever

Despite the money to be made from the trade in tulips, the bulbs were not part of the official commodities market, and florist traders gathered in taverns across the country to buy and sell. Sales were limited to the summer period when the bulbs were resting, a time when the blooms could not be seen. To overcome this problem, the painter and nurseryman Emanuel Sweerts came up with the novel concept of an illustrated catalog, *Florilegium Amplissimum et Selectissimum*, which was published in Frankfurt in 1612. The idea of a catalog was appealing, but as most growers were busily cultivating their own varieties, its use was limited. Some Dutch growers commissioned illustrated manuscripts of their own cultivars for use as a sales tool, although prices were not included.

By 1633 the scarcity of tulip bulbs was less of an issue than it had been. There was a plethora of new, exotically named cultivars. Estimates suggest 500 cultivars had been bred, some performing rather better than others. Growers sold the more run-of-the-mill cultivars at reduced prices and offloaded stock to peddlers for wider sale, opening up the market to new consumers. The following year, even the price of the run-of-the-mill bulbs was rising steadily and anyone who could afford it was investing. By 1636 the price was doubling in a week, and stories began to circulate that there were fortunes to be made in the trade of bulbs. This was gambling on a grand scale and as the prices of the most desirable varieties became prohibitive, the interest in trading the cheaper

bulbs increased. Growing numbers of people began raising whatever funds they could obtain to participate in this trade, working on the basis that in a few years of reinvestment they would accrue substantial profits.

While tulips were traditionally traded in the summer months, the trade in offsets from the mother bulb, which take several years to mature, was rather more flexible. By 1635, merchants were no longer trading the bulbs and offsets in their stores, but rather selling ones still in the ground on a speculative promise. Such offsets could not be supplied, of course, so instead a promissory note confirmed the sale, to be concluded when the offset was lifted.

Offsets were traded by their weight when planted, a system that gave some indication of the growing maturity of the bulb. In theory bulbs would weigh more when lifted, and therefore have more value. Bulbs were weighed in aces, and there were approximately 10,000 aces in a pound – amounts varied slightly from region to region. Promissory notes listed the cultivar, its weight and the date it would be lifted. This practice was technically illegal, but as the commodities market did not regulate the trade in bulbs, there were no measures in place to fix prices or to control methods of trading.

Experts could determine the quality of a bulb by looking at it, but in this new speculative market, the bulbs could not be inspected and indeed might not even exist. A buyer might not have the money to pay for the bulb in full, but could obtain a promissory note for a deposit, then sell the bulb at a profit. Full payment was due on the lifting and weighing of the bulb in the summer. Bulbs were thus changing hands repeatedly on the basis of promissory notes in a futures market. Moreover, as communication was poor there was no fixed price; the value of bulbs varied from town to town.

By the autumn of 1636, trading in tulips was frenetic. It has been estimated that at the peak of trading a single bulb could change hands ten times in one day. As each person traded successfully, they would encourage their nearest and dearest to do likewise.

A commonly quoted example is that of a red and yellow Switzer tulip bulb, which despite being sufficiently uninteresting to be sold by weight in aces, still managed to achieve a price of 60 guilders (approximately $900 today) per pound in the autumn of 1636. As the market moved towards its peak, the same Switzer was achieving 1,500 guilders per pound (approximately $22,500 today).

The mood changed at a florist's auction in Haarlem in early February 1637. Despite there being a good crowd, there was some indefinable shift. When the auctioneer offered bulbs at prices that had been reached just the day before, no bids were placed. Nor was interest piqued when these prices were reduced. The silence was deafening.

What induced this sudden show of caution is not known, but word of the market's collapse in Haarlem spread like wildfire and within days there was simply no longer a market for tulip bulbs. The trade that Clusius had despised had collapsed; the dealers were caught in a chain of debts and the debtors did not know how they could discharge their obligations. It is sometimes stated that tulip fever brought the Dutch economy to its knees, but in reality it did no such thing. However, of those who engaged in the trade, while some lucky people did make a fortune, the less fortunate remained in debt for the rest of their lives.

At the end of April 1637, the court of Holland decreed that the matter should be dealt with at a local level. All contracts were to be suspended while matters were investigated, and lawyers and notaries were told to stop issuing writs on any cases involving the trade of tulips. Only a small percentage of debtors were taken to court, although a backlog of disputes dragged on for some years. Many growers went out of business, but others survived and took advantage of the new business opportunities. The speculative bubble may have burst, but there was still plenty of interest in bulbs and the best of these changed hands, albeit more cautiously, for in excess of 300 guilders a piece (some $4,500 today). Tulips were even shipped to Turkey to feed a new passion for the plants generated by the Ottoman ruler Ahmet III (1673–1736), whose reign from 1703 to 1730 was dubbed the Tulip Era.

As news of the spectacular growth and collapse of the tulip market in the Dutch Republic spread across Europe, people wanted to see the flower for themselves and an export market sprang up. Dutch dominance of the market had never been seriously challenged, but tulip fanciers in Flanders, Britain and France worked assiduously to breed new cultivars. Even so, an exciting new development came again from the Netherlands; Jacob Heinrich Krelage (1824–1901) purchased a collection of tulips in 1885 from which he cultivated a new class called Darwin, introduced in 1889 at the World Exhibition in Paris. Tall and strong, the Darwin tulips caused another spike in tulip sales and were the stars of many a Victorian bedding scheme.

The same J.H. Krelage, possibly inspired by Alexandre Dumas' novel *The Black Tulip*, also introduced "La Tulipe Noire" in 1891. Published

in 1850, the novel told a story about the city of Haarlem offering a handsome prize for the growing of a black tulip, motivating many real-life growers towards the same ambition. "La Tulipe Noire" is not actually black, but rather dark purple in hue ('Paul Scherer,' introduced in 1997, is thought to be the darkest to date).

Tulips in the UK

In Britain, the first issue of *Curtis's Botanical Magazine* was published in 1787, with a print run of 3,000. Still published quarterly under the same name today, it was designed to introduce "the most ornamental foreign plants" to amateur enthusiasts. It featured beautiful and precise illustrations by artists who worked in conjunction with botanists at Kew Gardens to ensure accuracy. The magazine encouraged botanists and florists (the latter term referring to plant specialists who grew plants for pleasure) to focus on cultivating perfection in one kind of flower.

This new pastime for amateur growers was classless, and manual laborers embraced the concept with enthusiasm. Home-growing was actively encouraged, so anyone with a yard or community garden could participate. Florists' societies gathered for meetings in public houses to discuss the merits of various plants, to exchange seeds and bulbs, and to plan competitions. This system enabled men who could not normally afford tulip bulbs to engage in the breeding of new cultivars.

Coverage of the societies' work in the national and local press further stimulated interest, and by the mid-19th century florists' societies had sprung up all over the country. Philip Miller, Head Gardener at the Chelsea Physic Garden in London, noted the standard for English florists' tulips in 1724 in *The Gardener's and Florist's Dictionary*: "Tall strong stem. The bottom part of the flower should be proportioned to the top, the upper part rounded and not pointed and the stripes should be small and regular, arising quite from the bottom."

One of the most famous English florists was Tom Storer, a railway worker who cultivated his crop of tulips on railway embankments. He was responsible for the breeding of three new cultivars, 'Dr Hardy,' 'Sam Barlow' and 'Earl of Derby,' all named after fellow tulip-fanciers and patrons. Sam Barlow himself started life as an apprentice at Stakehill Bleach Works at Castleton and ended up as its proprietor. He spent a fortune building up a vast collection of English florists' tulips and was not averse to buying up the entire stock of a new cultivar so that no one else could claim to have it.

Membership of florists' societies slumped dramatically in the 1870s; the fact that the first-ever Football Association tournament took place in 1871–2 may be entirely coincidental. Only the Wakefield and North of England Tulip Society has survived. The Society has preserved the rare and historic bulbs, and still cultivates the prized breaking tulips. Spare bulbs of these are distributed among members of the society but are not available commercially, since the sale of bulbs infected by the breaking virus is now prohibited to stop cross-contamination.

Tulips today

Dutch growers still remain the masters in both tulip bulb cultivation and in the cut-flower market, despite English growers attempting to give them a run for their money from the late 19th century into the mid-20th century. Ultimately, they could not compete and even Americans import the majority of their tulips

from the Netherlands. Today almost half of the expanse of the Netherlands is given over to bulb fields, with half of that area used for the production of forced tulips. The Dutch produce almost two billion tulips annually and remain the world's leading exporter of flowers and bulbs.

The striped cultivars we see today are the product of centuries of hybridization, as genetic information from the latest successful introduction is crossed with the genes of another via pollination. Thousands of new cultivars have been introduced and tulips are nurtured in state-of-the-art facilities that replicate their ideal growing conditions. Despite the advancement in our understanding of this exceptional flower, the process of propagation is relatively unchanged. Breeders will use a paintbrush or tweezers to gently transfer the pollen from the anthers of one cultivar to the ovary of another. They will then harvest the seed and nurture it for six to seven years until the final result is revealed in the bloom.

From a hundred thousand such crosses a breeder may be lucky to get five worthy new cultivars. Imagine the excitement of the moment of discovery! But even then, breeders have to conduct tests to establish the viability of a cultivar and build up stock via offsets before the bulbs can be introduced to the market. They could still be beaten to the punch if another breeder has cultivated a similar bloom and manages to introduce it first. So when you next marvel at the beauty of a tulip, remember that it is the product of centuries of breeding and offer a salute to the efforts of the men and women throughout history who have labored to create the exquisite flower you see before you.

THE
CLASSIC
BLOOM

Mondial

This small, perfectly formed tulip bursts into life in mid-spring and produces exquisite, cupped, peony-like blooms. It buds green with creamy-white tips, opening to reveal snow-white papery petals that are etched at the inner base with a burst of canary yellow, giving the bloom a warm and sunny heart as though lit from within. The filaments are pale green topped by bright yellow anthers dusted with sulfur pollen, while the style is a curling, cream sculpture that emerges from the green ovary. The foliage is stiff and upright, supporting the flowers and helping them to withstand both winds and spring showers.

As 'Mondial' has a soft and pleasing perfume, plant it near the edges of paths and terraces so you can smell its fragrance while you admire its beauty.

Type Double Early
Flowering Mid-spring
Aspect Full sun
Soil Fertile, well-drained soil
Planting depth 7in (17cm)
Bulb spacing 4in (10cm)
Average height 8–12in (20–30cm)
Companion plants *Narcissus* 'Actaea' or *Myosotis sylvatica* (forget-me-not)
As a cut flower Very pretty, but short-stemmed
Forcing Yes
Similar varieties 'Global Desire' (Double Early), 'Mount Tacoma' (Double Late)

Flaming Margarita

This remarkably pretty tulip is a flounced and ruffled mass of white petals streaked with delicate raspberry feathering. Despite its feminine exuberance, it is a distinctly elegant tulip that will quietly outshine showier cultivars with its eye-catching beauty.

'Flaming Margarita' buds green and turns cream with pale pink feathering. As it matures, the petals turn white and the feathering, which appears from a sunshine-yellow basal blotch, darkens to an intense shade of raspberry sorbet. The anthers are yellow and the pistil is green, with a primrose-yellow cap. The petals curl right back, gradually evolving into a great saucer of a bloom. This tulip is simply wonderful as a cut flower in the house, where you can appreciate all its subtle nuances and gaze into its splendid interior.

Type Double Early
Flowering Mid-spring
Aspect Full sun
Soil Fertile, well-drained soil
Planting depth 7in (17cm)
Bulb spacing 4in (10cm)
Average height 12in (30cm)
Companion plants *Myosotis sylvatica* (white, pink or blue forget-me-not) or *Nigella damascena* (love-in-a-mist)
As a cut flower Superb; it is grown as a cutting flower
Forcing Yes
Similar varieties 'Danceline' (Double Late)

China Town

Employing all the subtlety of an artist's palette, 'China Town' mixes tones of moss green, pale lime, gray-green, shell pink and palest pink in an intricate and finely drawn masterpiece. The gray-green foliage is edged in white, a feature in itself, but as the green and white buds appear the stage is set to be transformed. The bloom is all elegance and sits on a stem that curves in a perfect arc to give a graceful aesthetic – there are no stiff uprights here. Green flames run up the petals, bleeding almost imperceptibly into a faint haze of yellow and apricot before turning pink. As the bloom matures the colors fade, and the petals are shot through with a faint buttery yellow. The pistil is dark green, topped by pale green curls, and the stamens are fine coppery strands. Despite its delicate appearance, this is a sturdy plant that flowers over a long period. Plant it at the front of borders, as edging alongside paths or in containers.

'China Town' was registered in 1988 by A.W. Captein & Son. It received a coveted Royal Horticultural Society Award of Garden Merit in 1995.

Type Viridiflora
Flowering Late spring
Aspect Full sun or partial shade
Soil Fertile, well-drained soil
Planting depth 8in (20cm)
Bulb spacing 4in (10cm)
Average height 12in (30cm)
Companion plants Perfect with soft pink tulips, or front it with *Stachys byzantina* (lamb's ear)
As a cut flower This has such subtle coloration that it will blend with almost anything and is delightfully wayward in stem
Forcing No
Similar varieties 'Flaming Spring Green,' a creamy-white, red and green Viridiflora

Apeldoorn

The ultimate classic garden tulip, 'Apeldoorn' glows with brilliant bold red, making a dramatic splash in the border. Combine this with its striking height and you have the tulip equivalent of a supermodel. However, 'Apeldoorn' is a grand old lady with a pedigree dating back to 1951, and its showy flowers and agreeable tendency of repeat flowering for a couple of years without being lifted have made it a firm garden favorite. Moreover, supported on sturdy stems, the blooms stand proud of the foliage and will take much battering from wind and rain without spoiling.

'Apeldoorn' buds green, then the petals become infused with a superb red – vivid, intense and warm. Every petal has a black basal blotch that is topped with a thin band of yellow. The stamens are inky black, and the pistil is a creamy pale yellow. As the giant flower opens it forms a beautiful, flat-topped cup shape that can reach 5in (13cm).

This Darwin Hybrid tulip was raised and introduced by D.W. Lefeber & Co in 1951. Lefeber, from Lisse in the Netherlands province of South Holland, created the first Darwin Hybrid in 1943 by crossing a Darwin Single Late with *Tulipa fosteriana* 'Madame Lefeber.'

Type Darwin Hybrid
Flowering Mid-spring
Aspect Full sun
Soil Fertile; 'Apeldoorn' flourishes in particularly well-drained soil
Planting depth 6–8in (15–20cm)
Bulb spacing 4–6in (10–15cm)
Average height 1ft 4in–1ft 8in (40–50cm)
Companion plants Mix with other Darwin Hybrids such as the glowing red and yellow *Tulipa* 'American Dream'
As a cut flower Spectacular
Forcing No
Similar varieties 'Acropolis,' with cherry-red flowers

Super Parrot

While most Parrot tulips celebrate color in all its splendid glories, 'Super Parrot' opts for a quieter color palette. The green-white buds emerge from fat whorls of wavy, gray-green foliage. As the bud breaks it reveals snow-white petals feathered with tongues of moss green, grass green, leaf green and yellow-green. The petals twist and curl into fantastic sculptural shapes, the edges torn, jagged, frayed and fringed like an elegant couture version of a rough punk finish. As the flower matures it spreads its white petals wide, like the wings of an exotic bird, and at the heart is a tiny green pistil topped with a jaunty lemon cap and a ring of sulfur-yellow stamens. The whole effect is very pretty and distinctly upmarket.

'Super Parrot' was registered by the Dutch breeders M. Boots Bloembollenselectie B.V. in 1998.

Type Parrot
Flowering Mid to late spring
Aspect Full sun
Soil Fertile, well-drained soil
Planting depth 7in (17cm)
Bulb spacing 4in (10cm)
Average height 1ft 4in (40cm)
Companion plants *Leucojum aestivum* (summer snowflake) or plant amid the superb foliage of *Euphorbia characias*
As a cut flower Extremely classy
Forcing No
Similar varieties 'White Parrot' also has green feathering, but the petals are less frayed

Tulipa tarda

This diminutive tulip is a perfect example of the extraordinary diversity of the genus. Hailing from Tien Shan – the Mountains of Heaven – in Central Asia, in the right spot it will flower year after year and self-seed happily, so your stock will expand. It buds pink-green and breaks to reveal flashes of white and yellow. When fully open the bloom is so vibrant it appears sulfur yellow at first glance, but the petals are white-tipped with a large yellow flame extending from the base. The stamens and pistil are also yellow, producing a bright and sunny flower. The blooms hug the ground, but occasionally can reach 8in (20cm) in height. Each one can throw out as many as eight flowers from an encircling ring of leaves that are a perfect foil for its vivid coloration. This tulip is also blessed with a delicious honeyed fragrance, but you'll have to get down on your hands and knees to appreciate it.

T. tarda was given the Royal Horticultural Society Award of Garden Merit in 1993, and as its name hints it flowers late in the season. Given its provenance, *T. tarda* fares well if you pay particular attention to drainage, incorporating some grit into the surrounding soil when you plant it at the front of a flower bed or in containers such as troughs.

Type Species
Flowering Late spring
Aspect Full sun
Soil Fertile, well-drained soil
Planting depth 4in (10cm)
Bulb spacing 3in (7.5cm)
Average height 2–4in (5–10cm)
Companion plants Let it shine alone
As a cut flower Short-stemmed, so best left *in situ*
Forcing No
Similar varieties *Tulipa turkestanica* is a little taller and the flowers are white with a yellow heart

TULIPA ORPHANIDEA HAGERI [left], TULIPA TARDA [above]

APRICOT BEAUTY [above], DAYDREAM [right]

Danceline

As delicate in appearance as a piece of painted porcelain but surprisingly sturdy of stem and obligingly easy to grow, this exquisite flower looks equally good in both border and vase. 'Danceline' buds a feathered green but opens to reveal a petticoat of creamy-white petals, all tipped and sometimes splashed with delicate brush strokes of raspberry pink. The outer petals are cream and feathered prettily with green. As the flower matures it explodes into a stupendous peony-like bloom, and the petals flush faintly with pink. The anthers are yellow, but the petals curl over them discreetly until full maturity.

While this is a strong-stemmed tulip, it does best in a sheltered situation because of the weight of its head. It was registered by Vertuco B.V. in 2006.

Type Double Late
Flowering Late spring
Aspect Full sun or partial shade
Soil Fertile, well-drained soil
Planting depth 6–7in (15–17cm)
Bulb spacing 4in (10cm)
Average height 1ft 5in–1ft 8in (44–50cm)
Companion plants *Myosotis alpestris* 'White' (forget-me-not) or *Alchemilla mollis*
As a cut flower Excellent
Forcing No
Similar varieties 'Toucan,' a white single with petals bordered in pink, or 'Flaming Margarita'

FOXTROT [above], NEGRITA [right]

Greenland

The coloration on this pink and green tulip is so delicate that each petal looks as though it has been shaded by hand with a fine crayon to create a pattern of tiny lines. As the green buds break they reveal slivers of pale pink. The bloom is sugar pink, with the trademark green Viridiflora flame running from the base to the tip of each petal. As the flower matures its tones mellow; the green stripe yellows and the pink warms in tone. The interior of the flower is exquisite, with tongues of soft green or pale sunset-yellow offset with rosy pink and hints of peach. The stamens are long and black and the pistil is a creamy ruffled sculpture.

'Greenland,' otherwise known as 'Groenland,' is an established cultivar that was raised by J.F. van den Berg & Sons, registered in 1955 and is still going strong.

Type Viridiflora
Flowering Late spring
Aspect Full sun
Soil Fertile, well-drained soil
Planting depth 7in (17cm)
Bulb spacing 4in (10cm)
Average height 1ft 6in (45cm)
Companion plants *Lunaria rediviva*
As a cut flower Gorgeous and long-lasting
Forcing No
Similar varieties 'Virichic'

Ollioules

This is a tulip of many moods, with an incandescent beauty that shifts in shape and color as it matures. From a green bud a tight flower emerges, the petals sugary pink, fading to white at the edges. But then it opens into a perfect cupped flower and as it does so the color palette shifts, the pink becoming warm and fleshy while the white border extends so that the bloom appears to be lit from within. As the petals revert further still their interior color bleaches out into the faintest tones of pale green, pale pink and white. At the center of this now full-bodied, ragged-petaled bloom, biscuit-colored filaments are topped with pert black anthers that guard the pale green, lemon-capped pistil. As well as these charming color combinations, 'Ollioules' is also blessed with a delightful fragrance.

Despite its delicate appearance, 'Ollioules' stands on tall, sturdy stems and can withstand rain and wind. This tulip was introduced in 1988 by Van Zanten Brothers and it received the Royal Horticultural Society Award of Garden Merit in 1999.

Type Darwin Hybrid
Flowering Mid to late spring
Aspect Full sun or partial shade
Soil Fertile, well-drained soil
Planting depth 7in (17cm)
Bulb spacing 4in (10cm)
Average height 1ft 8in–2ft (50–60cm)
Companion plants *Myosotis alpestris* 'White' (forget-me-not)
As a cut flower Extraordinarily beautiful; mix it with *Tulipa* 'La Belle Époque' if you get the chance
Forcing No
Similar varieties None

Queen of Night

Dark, luscious, glossy and indubitably stylish, 'Queen of Night' is an absolute temptress of a tulip. This simple six-petaled bloom has a beautifully classic line and is an intense shade of aubergine that complements other tulips, yet demands attention in the flower bed and vase. 'Queen of Night' buds a greenish-purple, but when fully open in all her inky glory the color of the petals is the perfect foil for dark red, rusty orange, apricot and copper tulips, but is also very pretty with soft pink, violet and white. The pale creamy-white pistil has a purplish-black cap. As the green leaves are short, the flower heads stand proud of their foliage. In a vase, this tulip droops attractively.

'Queen of Night' was raised by J.J. Grullemans & Sons, reputedly in 1944. The nursery was beaten to the punch in the quest for a "black" tulip by C. Keur & Sons, who registered the magnificent 'Black Parrot' in 1937. A true black tulip is yet to be cultivated – the search has been on since the bulbs first arrived in Europe in the 16th century – but these dark purple tulips are utterly seductive.

Type Single Late
Flowering Late spring
Aspect Full sun
Soil Fertile, well-drained soil
Planting depth 4–6in (10–15cm)
Bulb spacing 4in (10cm)
Average height 2ft (60cm)
Companion plants *Tulipa* 'Rasta Parrot,' *T.* 'Foxy Foxtrot,' *T.* 'La Belle Époque,' *T.* 'Black Parrot,' or *Camassia* 'Blue Heaven'
As a cut flower Combine with pink or orange tulips for stunning effect
Forcing No
Similar varieties 'Black Hero' is the same color but a double

Sapporo

It is perhaps the subtly evolving coloration that makes 'Sapporo' one of a kind. It buds green, turns a pale lemony yellow, then fades as it unfurls to a creamy buttermilk or even white through a long flowering period. The blooms have a particularly clean and precise Lily-flowered form and hold a tight, upright and elegant shape before the petals curl back to reveal more of the heart. The stamen and pistil are sulfur yellow and the merest hints of yellow remain in the petals so that it complements other yellow flowers, providing a cool accent but not standing out as a shade apart. The flowers are wonderfully long-lasting.

'Sapporo' was introduced in 1992 by M. Boots, a flower bulb company in the Netherlands that breeds new cultivars.

Type Lily-flowered
Flowering Late spring
Aspect Full sun
Soil Fertile, well-drained soil
Planting depth 4–6in (10–15cm)
Bulb spacing 3in (7.5cm)
Average height 1ft 6in (45cm)
Companion plants Glorious with an underplanting of blues such as *Muscari* (grape hyacinth)
As a cut flower Mixes beautifully with yellow blooms
Forcing No
Similar varieties 'Greenstar' is a white Lily-flowered tulip with green flames

SAPPORO [above], MOUNT TACOMA [right]

La Belle Époque

This is a charming tulip with a sensuous and sophisticated coloring, reminiscent of the soft tones of 1930s silk lingerie. 'La Belle Époque' buds green, the outer petals flushed on the rear with a beautiful, deep dusty pink, tipped in the center with green. As the bloom unfurls it reveals heart-shaped petals with an interior palette infused with soft shades of coffee, apricot, copper and lemon, the color darkening and intensifying toward the base of each petal. As it matures the colors fade to cream, lemon and white with flushes of pale pink, warm pink and violet, and the interior of the bloom reveals black stamens.

The flowers are long-lasting in the border and sensational in a vase. This variety blends wonderfully with other tulips, especially deep, dark purples, whites, creams and pinks. The blue-green leaves are deliciously wavy. The color palette varies slightly from bulb to bulb and according to location: some are more buff in tone, some are pinker.

'La Belle Époque' was registered in 2011 by Vertuco B.V., a tulip grower from the Netherlands.

Type Double Early
Flowering Mid to late spring
Aspect Full sun or partial shade
Soil Fertile, well-drained soil
Planting depth 5–6in (13–15cm)
Bulb spacing 4in (10cm)
Average height 1ft 4in (40cm)
Companion plants Plant with other tulips such as 'Queen of Night' or 'Montreux,' or ring with *Anemone blanda*
As a cut flower Stunning, and mixes well with other white, pink and dark purple tulips
Forcing No
Similar varieties A one-off

White Triumphator

It's hard to find a more elegant tulip than 'White Triumphator' and it's a reliable performer, too, long-lasting in the garden and in the vase, which perhaps accounts for its longevity; it has been on sale for more than 60 years. It buds green, rapidly turning to a warm, buttery cream, but blooms an immaculate snow-white. The long stamens are yellow, and the pistil is green. The flower heads stand proud of the foliage, and because of its height 'White Triumphator' benefits from a sheltered site. The late Christopher Lloyd, the inspirational garden writer and creator of the magnificent garden at Great Dixter in East Sussex, described 'White Triumphator' as "strikingly handsome" and observed that it not only held its own in the flower bed, but multiplied.

'White Triumphator' was introduced in 1942 by Van Tubergen. It received the Royal Horticultural Society Award of Garden Merit in 1995.

Type Lily-flowered
Flowering Late spring
Aspect Full sun
Soil Fertile, well-drained soil
Planting depth 4–6in (10–15cm)
Bulb spacing 4in (10cm)
Average height 1ft 8in (50cm)
Companion plants Works well with all colors of tulip, but it is so tall it can stand behind the leafy clumps of herbaceous perennials such as daylilies (*Hemerocallis*), which will flower a little later
As a cut flower Exquisite
Forcing No
Similar varieties 'Greenstar' is a white Lily-flowered tulip with green flames, or opt for the Single Early 'White Marvel'

THE OPULENT FLOWER

Abba

Fully open, Abba is a ruffled can-can dancer's petticoat of a bloom. There is something indefinably joyful about this ravishing, compact scarlet tulip, which buds green, unfurling to reveal a glorious mass of vivid petals that form a wonderful goblet. As the green recedes from the outer petals it initially leaves little slashes of yellow. The petals at the heart of the flower have sunny, yellow basal blotches and the pistil is ringed by inky-black stamens. In a vase it has a relaxed easy-going style, drooping happily to form delightfully laid-back arrangements, and it is also blessed with a lovely fragrance.

As Abba is small it is a perfect tulip for pots, where it will joyfully herald the arrival of spring, although its heavy flower heads make it inclined to droop in the wind and rain. It was registered in 1978 by Bakker Bros in the Netherlands.

Type Double Early
Flowering Early to mid spring
Aspect Full sun
Soil Fertile, well-drained soil
Planting depth 7in (17cm)
Bulb spacing 4in (10cm)
Average height 8–12in (20–30cm)
Companion plants Grape hyacinth (*Muscari*)
As a cut flower An absolute joy
Forcing Yes
Similar varieties 'Red Baby Doll' is a darker hue and taller

Exquisit

Boasting great saucer-shaped blooms packed with ruffled petals, this Double Late tulip has huge and distinctive presence. Apart from its unusual shade of eminence purple, 'Exquisit' emerges from the bud looking more like an artichoke than a flower. The fat, bright green buds are tipped with pink as they break and a tight cone of perfectly arranged purple petals peep up above a protective shell of green sepals. The bloom erupts upwards and outwards until it resembles a beautiful cupped peony and as it matures the color fades and warms to mulberry. The petals are tipped white at the base, the style is pink, topped with a yellow stigma, and the stamens are yellow.

'Exquisit' was registered by Q.J. Vink & Zn B.V. in 2013.

Type Double Late
Flowering Late spring
Aspect Full sun or partial shade
Soil Fertile, well-drained soil
Planting depth 4in (10cm)
Bulb spacing 4in (10cm)
Average height 1ft 4in–1ft 8in (40–50cm)
Companion plants Tuck it behind clumps of geraniums: the chocolaty *G. phaeum* var. *phaeum* 'Samobor,' the violet *G. phaeum* 'Lily Lovell,' or the white *G. pratense* 'Double Jewel'
As a cut flower Rich and sumptuous
Forcing Yes
Similar varieties One of a kind

SUNSET MIAMI [above], TOM POUCE [right]

Monsella

Despite its diminutive size, 'Monsella' is the extrovert of the flower bed with its whopping blooms in irrepressibly cheerful primary colors. It buds green with hints of yellow and explodes into huge, bowl-shaped, yellow flowers with a diameter of 5–6in (13–15cm), all decorated with red stripes and splashes and the odd streak of white or green. The petals open flat in the sun, revealing a green style with a sculpted primrose stigma and sandy-brown stamens. Each flower is different from its neighbor, but all petals bear a fine red stripe from base to tip. *En masse*, 'Monsella' puts on a dazzling show like dancers at the Rio Carnival and as each bulb throws up three blooms you get plenty of bang for your buck. It's fabulous in the flower bed, the flowerpot and the vase.

'Monsella' was registered in 1981 by Bakker Bros in the Netherlands.

Type Double Early
Flowering Early to mid spring
Aspect Full sun and partial shade
Soil Fertile, well-drained soil
Planting depth 7in (17cm)
Bulb spacing 4in (10cm)
Average height 8–12in (20–30cm)
Companion plants Plant with yellow and red tulips for a dazzling spring display
As a cut flower Excellent
Forcing Yes
Similar varieties 'Banja Luka'

Banja Luka

There is nothing subtle about this vibrant and dynamic tulip, a swirl of primary colors so bright it almost hurts to look at it. The tightly folded green bud turns pale yellow without a hint of the glories to come, then breaks into a neatly proportioned yellow tulip with petals edged in fine red lines. It is as the bloom expands that its full magnificent impact is revealed, each petal daubed with the brightest, boldest red feathering on a hot yellow base. Viewed from above, it is a magnificent swirling ball of red and yellow. In the sunshine the colors from the petals merge together to add orange to the psychedelic effect. En masse it is like procession of flaming torches. Peep into the heart and you'll see inky-black basal blotches, a green style topped with a cream tricorn cap and inky-black stamens.
Plant it in containers or a dull spot in the border and wait for the explosion of color.

'Banja Luka' was registered in 1998 by the Dutch company MTS Houtman & Konijn.

Type Darwin Hybrid
Flowering Mid to late spring
Aspect Full sun or partial shade
Soil Fertile, well-drained soil
Planting depth 7in (17cm)
Bulb spacing 4in (10cm)
Average height 1ft 8in (50cm)
Companion plants Let it stand out in a mass of greenery from other herbaceous perennials yet to flower
As a cut flower Dazzling
Forcing Yes
Similar varieties 'Monsella' is equally bright, but with a higher proportion of yellow than red

Gavota

The spring garden is inclined toward a yellow-and-white color scheme, with daffodils, forsythia, primroses and crocus all bursting forth. If the garden is yellow-heavy it can be hard to know which tulips to plant for the best color. 'Gavota,' a tall, elegant tulip, offers both perfect harmony and a diverting color accent. Budding greeny-purple, the flower opens to reveal petals etched in burgundy red, darker at the base, that bleed into a buttery, cream-and-white tip. When the flower fully opens it is magnificently drawn; a white flash from the tip of each inner petal descends to meet the burgundy flame and the yellow border on close inspection has hints of canary, primrose and sunshine. Each petal carries a bright yellow basal blotch and there's a green style with a tricorn primrose-yellow stigma at the heart, ringed by yellow filaments with inky-black anthers.

'Gavota' was registered in 1995 by Bloembollenbureau Cebeco, a bulb nursery in the Netherlands. It was given the Royal Horticultural Society Award of Garden Merit in 2010.

Type Triumph
Flowering Late spring
Aspect Full sun
Soil Fertile, well-drained soil
Planting depth 7in (17cm)
Bulb spacing 4in (10cm)
Average height 1ft 4in–1ft 8in (40–50cm)
Companion plants *Alchemilla mollis*, white narcissus and wallflowers such as *Erysimum cheiri* 'Sunset Primrose'
As a cut flower A superb accent mixed in with yellow, cream, white and greens
Forcing Yes
Similar varieties One of a kind

Orange Favourite

Blessed with a heady perfume offering a hint of freesia and spice, this exquisite sorbet of a flower is garlanded with delicate tints of color – its name simply does not do it justice. As a newly opened bud it gleams in warm coppery-orange tones with multi-hued flames of violet, damson, moss green, crimson and raspberry streaking across the petals. As the ragged-tipped petals mature and spread the colors soften and fade to shell pink, rose pink, flesh pink, peach, apricot and coral mixed in with butter and sage green, but the heart continues to glow warmly. Peep inside and you'll see a green style topped with a butter-yellow stigma, all ringed by inky stamens.

Plant 'Orange Favourite' in the border or in containers, where its warm color palette will give you a huge boost in the spring. It was registered in 1930 by the Dutch grower K.C. Vooren.

Type Parrot
Flowering Late spring
Aspect Full sun
Soil Fertile, well-drained soil
Planting depth 7in (17cm)
Bulb spacing 4in (10cm)
Average height 1ft 4in–1ft 8in (40–50cm)
Companion plants The feathery leaves of common or bronze fennel (*Foeniculum vulgare* or *F. vulgare* 'Purpureum') are a perfect backdrop and *Allium hollandicum* 'Purple Sensation' will add sculptural shapes as it prepares to bloom
As a cut flower Mix it with opulent shades of red, purple, orange and yellow
Forcing Yes
Similar varieties 'Blumex Favourite' is brighter still

Peach Blossom

This feminine ruffle of a tulip has been enhancing gardens for more than 125 years. It buds green, opening to reveal creamy-white petals finely etched along the borders with a mass of rose-pink lines and tipped here and there with streaks of green. As the bloom matures, color washes the petals to a deeper shade of pink, although it fades to white towards the yellow basal blotch. The pistil is green topped with a butter-yellow star and the stamens are sulfur yellow. Small in size, this charming tulip is eminently suitable for pots and window boxes or for placing to the forefront of flower beds.

'Peach Blossom' was registered in 1890 by H.N. van Leeuwen.

Type Double Early
Flowering Early to mid spring
Aspect Full sun
Soil Fertile, well-drained soil
Planting depth 7in (17cm)
Bulb spacing 4in (10cm)
Average height 10–12in (25–30cm)
Companion plants *Myosotis alpestris* (forget-me-not) and white pansies
As a cut flower Ravishing with white, pink and blue
Forcing Yes
Similar varieties 'Foxtrot' (Double Early) or 'Angélique' (Double Late)

Foxy Foxtrot

Fragrant 'Foxy Foxtrot' is a soft watercolor wash of yellow, orange, apricot, pink, cream, white and green hues that combine to make it glow like a pale spring sunrise. The soft richness of its color palette ensures that it can act as a mood-changer in the flower bed, harmonizing with oranges, yellows and purples. Budding green, it opens into a creamy butter-yellow goblet streaked with green, peach, apricot, white and pink. As it matures the petals stretch wide to form a shallow cup and are etched with fine lines of orange, coral and apricot that intensify in color and flood them. At its heart stand a green pistil and green anthers. The wavy-edged foliage is blue-green in color.

'Foxy Foxtrot' was registered in 2011 by Vertuco B.V.

Type Double Early
Flowering Mid spring
Aspect Full sun
Soil Fertile, well-drained soil
Planting depth 7in (17cm)
Bulb spacing 4in (10cm)
Average height 1ft 4in–1ft 8in (40–50cm)
Companion plants Plant with *Tulipa* 'La Belle Époque' and *T.* 'Queen of Night'
As a cut flower Lights up the room and mixes well with a range of colors
Forcing Yes
Similar varieties 'Sunset Miami' has similar but stronger colors

Green Wave

This bloom is blessed with all the grace and style of a prima ballerina and is undeniably, impossibly lovely. 'Green Wave' has elongated, rippling buds in apple green and gray-green that undulate and swell as though something were trying to escape. As the bud unfurls the raggedy green petals gradually reveal a serrated rose-pink and raspberry border that bleeds into buttercream and thence into the central cocktail of green feathering – a mix of grass green, apple green, moss green and pine green. As the bloom matures it turns into a thing of transcendental beauty, an ephemeral sculpture of semi-translucent petals that unfurl to reveal a swirl of rippling and undulating pale pinks, cream, white and soft green. At the heart of the tattered bloom is a pale green pistil topped by an ornate stigma as pretty as one of the late Queen Mother's hats. This is ringed by delicate, inky-black stamens that add the final, beautiful flourish. Plant 'Green Wave' in a sheltered spot, as its large flower heads can be damaged by wind and rain.

'Green Wave' was introduced by J.J. Rozenbroek in 1984.

Type Parrot
Flowering Late spring
Aspect Full sun
Soil Fertile, well-drained soil
Planting depth 7in (17cm)
Bulb spacing 4in (10cm)
Average height 1ft 10in (55cm)
Companion plants Keep things simple; ring it with green herbaceous plants not yet in bloom, or mix it with airy, white spring flowers such as *Leucojum* and *Narcissus* 'Thalia,' and pale pink *Allium roseum bulbiferum*
As a cut flower An absolute vision, whether solo or mixed with other pink and white blooms, and it lasts well in the vase
Forcing Yes
Similar varieties One of a kind

Black Parrot

Statuesque and irrefutably elegant, this is a fashionista's bloom with pleated and folded satiny petals as artful as the finest Fortuny gown. Budding sage green, the finely cut petals ooze hints of damson as the bud prepares to break, when a shimmering mass of richly purple petals unfurl in tones of blackberry, sloe, elderberry and claret. The interior of the petal is even darker in hue, and in its shadowy heart all you will be able to spot is the creamy-white pistil. The sombre tones and rippling petals of 'Black Parrot' set it apart from all other tulips. To appreciate its regal beauty, place it where it can stand out from other colors, rather than blend into a shadowy background.

'Black Parrot' was registered in 1938 by C. Keur & Sons. It was given the Royal Horticultural Society Award of Garden Merit in 1995.

Type Parrot
Flowering Late spring
Aspect Full sun
Soil Fertile, well-drained soil
Planting depth 7in (17cm)
Bulb spacing 4in (10cm)
Average height 1ft 8in (50cm)
Companion plants *Tulipa* 'Copper Image' or *T.* 'Uncle Tom'
As a cut flower Fabulous solo, but even better with other pink or copper tulips, or a colorful riot of wallflowers (*Erysimum*)
Forcing Yes
Similar varieties 'Black Hero' has a similar intensity of color but is a Double Late

Hermitage

Rising on slender purple stems, 'Hermitage' is an absolute jewel of a tulip with a perfectly elegant and simple flower that is a flaming mass of sunset colors. Budding a greeny-purple, it opens to a ravishing, upright bloom. From a hint of yellow at the base, damson flames lick the petals which are washed in diffused shades of coral, salmon, rose pink, butter, sulfur yellow, apricot, violet, pale green and a warm coppery-orange that together have all the subtlety and Technicolor brilliance of J.M.W. Turner's painting *The Fighting Temeraire*. Like the best glowing sunset, it combines different elements of the color spectrum in such a way that despite its vivacity all is harmony too. Make sure you peep into the heart to see the blue anthers. Strong and sturdy, this tulip performs well in both border and container and is a good candidate for forcing.

'Hermitage' was registered in 1986 by Jan de Wit & Sons, a Dutch tulip grower for almost 100 years.

Type Triumph
Flowering Mid to late spring
Aspect Full sun
Soil Fertile, well-drained soil
Planting depth 7in (17cm)
Bulb spacing 4in (10cm)
Average height 1ft 2in (35cm)
Companion plants Plant near purple sage (*Salvia purpurea*), *Euphorbia* 'Nothowlee' ('Blackbird'), or *Euphorbia griffithii* 'Fireglow'; throw in some dark purple and deep pink tulips for good measure
As a cut flower Fabulous mixed with purple, dark red and pink
Forcing Yes
Similar varieties 'Hermitage Double,' the same but with double the petals, and 'Prinses Irene'

Parrot Negrita

Like a 1950s couture ball gown, this magnificent tulip explodes from a slender stem into a expansive skirt of pleated and ruffled petals in a seductively intense shade of purple-red. As the green bud breaks, beetroot flames creep up the bud and damson curls spill from the sides. It develops into a frothy, frilly confection of curled, twisted, raggedy-edged glossy petals. These ripple with color; damson, magenta, violet and aubergine can be seen in the peaks and troughs of each curling petal. As it matures the bloom spreads its shapely petals wide, revealing a pale-violet heart, containing a sculpted green pistil ringed by sulfur-yellow stamens. Mix it with dark purple, pink, orange and copper tulips in the flower bed.

'Parrot Negrita' was introduced in 2011 by Holland Bolroy Markt B.V., a Dutch company which specializes in the introduction of new tulip cultivars to the market.

Type Parrot
Flowering Mid to late spring
Aspect Full sun
Soil Fertile, well-drained soil
Planting depth 7in (17cm)
Bulb spacing 4in (10cm)
Average height 1ft 8in (50cm)
Companion plants Pink, blue, white or chocolate geraniums
As a cut flower A magnificent spectacle
Forcing Yes
Similar varieties 'Black Parrot' is a darker purple and 'Blue Parrot' is violet in hue

Uncle Tom

This is a drop-dead gorgeous tulip that produces exquisite, fragrant blooms that beg to be picked and brought into the house for arrangements. If you have the space it is worth cultivating it in serried ranks as a cutting flower, as well as popping it in containers and the border. The round green buds open to produce neat, cupped blooms full of tidily ruffled petals in a rich cardinal red. As the bud breaks the outer petals are streaked prettily in green before flooding with color. Here and there, at the very tips of the petals, there may be occasional hints of white, neatly emphasizing their polished, glossy finish. It is the intense color of its peony-like petals that makes 'Uncle Tom' so desirable and has helped ensure its longevity, for it is versatile enough to blend with darker purples, rich oranges and coppers or pale pinks. 'Uncle Tom' modestly conceals its heart, but if you get a glimpse you'll see a bright yellow interior, complete with a pale green sculpted pistil and violet anthers. Like all double tulips it is susceptible to damage from the wind and rain, so plant it in a sheltered situation.

'Uncle Tom' was registered by Zocher & Co. but has no formal listed date of introduction with the Royal General Bulb Growers' Association (KAVB), which is the international cultivar registration authority of all bulbous, cormous and tuberous-rooted plants. It was reputedly introduced around 1939.

Type Double Late
Flowering Late spring
Aspect Full sun
Soil Fertile, well-drained soil
Planting depth 6in (15cm)
Bulb spacing 4–5in (10–13cm)
Average height 1ft 6in (45cm)
Companion plants *Tulipa* 'Angélique'
As a cut flower Mesmerizing and seductive
Forcing Yes
Similar varieties 'Black Hero' is a darker damson

Black Hero

If you want drama and intensity in the flower bed then look no further than 'Black Hero.' In the long quest for a black tulip, 'Black Hero' comes very close, and is certainly one of the darkest tulips on the market. Of course it is not actually black at all, but the most sumptuous dark, glossy purple. It buds greeny-purple with hints of damson showing as the outer petals turn from green to plum. This is a fat bud like a peony that struggles to contain masses of glossy, satiny petals. As the flower opens it reveals shades of black cherry, sloe, burgundy and plum in the sunlight. It modestly conceals the pale green, white-capped pistil and dusty brown stamens behind its petals, but keep an eye out for a hint of the starry, white basal decoration. The bloom is a great tiered goblet of perfectly positioned petals, and its rich tone makes it the perfect foil for other tulips, be they white, pink, orange, rust or purple. It grows well in a container, but for full impact it looks most stunning growing with other shades in the border, or placed with blooms of other colors in a vase.

'Black Hero' was registered in 1984 by J. Beerepoot. It is a sport of 'Queen of Night.'

Type Double Late
Flowering Mid to late spring
Aspect Full sun
Soil Fertile, well-drained soil
Planting depth 6–8in (15–20cm)
Bulb spacing 6in (15cm)
Average height 2ft (60cm)
Companion plants Virtually any color of tulip or any herbaceous perennials, bar yellow
As a cut flower Apart from its showy good looks, 'Black Hero' will blend with almost any other color in a vase
Forcing Yes
Similar varieties 'Queen of Night' is a similar color, but single

THE
MOSAIC
BEAUTY

Blumex Favourite

Budding a gray-green, 'Blumex Favourite' undergoes a dramatic transformation as the bud matures, for the outer petals are infused with all the tones of the sunset; gray, violet, yellow and red. And, as if all this Technicolor glory were not enough, the reverse of the petals is tightly folded and curled like the fleece of an astrakhan lamb. This is an absolute showstopper of a tulip! As the petals unfurl they reveal a bold red interior, tipped initially with yellow, orange and green, hues that disappear as the flower fully opens. In a vase 'Blumex Favourite' is the personification of flamboyant drama, and the blooms are blessed with a faint, fruity fragrance.

Planted in the right conditions, this tulip blooms readily. It has sturdy stems, but like all Parrot tulips benefits from a sheltered site. On the downside, this is one of those cultivars that does not repeat flower efficiently, and it is best treated as an annual. 'Blumex Favourite' is a sport of 'Rococo'; it was registered by Fa. van Dam in 1992.

Type Parrot
Flowering Late spring
Aspect Full sun
Soil Fertile, well-drained soil
Planting depth 6–8in (15–20cm)
Bulb spacing 6in (15cm)
Average height 1ft 4in–1ft 8in (40–50cm)
Companion plants *Muscari* (grape hyacinth)
As a cut flower Superb
Forcing Difficult
Similar varieties 'Rococo'

Estella Rijnveld

Red and white flowers mixed together in a bouquet are said to symbolize blood and tears and are thought to be an unlucky combination. Superstition aside, there is often something indefinably tacky about this crude color mix. However, when red and white are combined in 'Estella Rijnveld' the effect is sensational. This tulip is all flamboyant drama. It buds a greeny-damson purple, and as the bud loosens curls of pale green and raspberry escape confinement. As the bloom opens it unleashes crimped and waved creamy-white petals sporting vivid scarlet flames, small tongues of sage and moss green and demure splashes of pale pink. The edges of each petal zig-zag as though trimmed with a blunt pair of pinking shears. The cupped blooms, which stand on short, sturdy stems, are very large and can reach 7in (17cm) in diameter. Peer inside the heart and you'll find a yellow-capped pistil and inky-black stamens. This is pure drama in the flower bed.

'Estella Rijnveld' was raised by De Mol, who rather alarmingly cultivated mutations in tulip and hyacinth bulbs with the aid of radiation. The tulips were on trial with Seger Brothers, in Lille on the French border with Belgium. In 1950 Segers Brothers presented the tulip to De Mol's wife Estella on her 70th birthday; her maiden name had been Rijnveld. It is hard to imagine a more wonderful gift. Segers Brothers registered the tulip in 1954. 'Estella Rijnveld' is also known as 'Gay Presto.'

Type Parrot
Flowering Mid spring
Aspect Full sun
Soil Fertile, well-drained soil
Planting depth 7in (17cm)
Bulb spacing 4in (10cm)
Average height 1ft 8in (50cm)
Companion plants *Lunaria annua* (honesty) or *Narcissus* 'Thalia'
As a cut flower Excellent
Forcing No
Similar varieties 'Carnaval de Nice' and 'Happy Generation' for color, although neither are Parrot tulips so they lack the distinctive Parrot form

Ravana

Budding green, the petals of this tulip gradually flood a warm canary yellow. As the green recedes it reveals damson flames that fade as the bloom matures, leaving a faint maroon stain on the center of the petals. At the heart of the cupped bloom is a pale green pistil topped with a cream cap and inky-black stamens. This tulip is also blessed with a sweet fragrance. This is a fabulously sunny tulip, but take care not to mix it with other greeny-yellows – it warrants a strong companion planting that will enhance its warm color palette.

'Ravana' was registered by Paul van Bentem Bloembollen B.V., in 2012. It is a strain of the orange and plum-colored 'Prinses Irene,' spotted among the sunset tones of that variety blooming in the bulb fields.

Type Triumph
Flowering Mid to late spring
Aspect Full sun or partial shade
Soil Fertile, well-drained soil
Planting depth 4–6in (10–15cm)
Bulb spacing 3in (7.5cm)
Average height 12in (30cm)
Companion plants *Tulipa* 'Queen of Night' or maroon and rust wallflowers (*Erysimum*)
As a cut flower A wonderfully rich color combination
Forcing No
Similar varieties 'Washington' is a similarly sunny yellow but has scarlet flames

Happy Generation

This beautiful tulip bears delicately painted flames on a white background and is utterly charming, especially when offset by white flowers. It buds first green, then white etched with little dashes of red. As the bloom expands the scarlet flames, all etched with hints of yellow, spread across each petal from base to tip. It matures into a magnificent, ragged-edged bowl of a flower, and when fully open the heart is a great swirl of red and white, with a large sulfur-yellow basal blotch. Even the foliage is pretty – each leaf is finely trimmed with silvery-white. This is a strong and sturdy hybrid that will withstand the worst the weather can throw at it.

'Happy Generation' was registered in 1988 by J. de Vries & Sons in the Netherlands.

Type Triumph
Flowering Mid to late spring
Aspect Full sun
Soil Fertile, well-drained soil
Planting depth 4in (10cm)
Bulb spacing 4in (10cm)
Average height 1ft 8in (50cm)
Companion plants Ring it with white *Narcissus*, *Leucojum* or *Myosotis alpestris* 'White' (forget-me-not)
As a cut flower Let it shine out among white flowers
Forcing Yes
Similar varieties 'Ice Follies,' another Triumph tulip, is white with red flames, and has a green pistil and stamens

Flaming Parrot

As wild and brazen as a Rio Carnival costume, this tulip is an absolute showstopper in the flower bed. Budding a fat green sculpture with tiny flames of yellow and scarlet, it explodes into a great undulating frou-frou of a flower. The canary-yellow petals, frayed and torn at the edges, are patterned with wayward streaks and dashes of crimson, offset with little tongues of moss green. The petals curl and twist this way and that, creating a frilly whimsy of color. As the bloom matures the yellow pales to a rich buttery-cream, each petal finely shaded at its extremities with dull salmon pink and scarlet in a multi-layered work of art. When the petals fully revert you'll find inky-black stamens and a white-capped pistil.

'Flaming Parrot' was introduced in 1968 by C.A. Verdegaal.

Type Parrot
Flowering Mid spring
Aspect Full sun
Soil Fertile, well-drained soil
Planting depth 7in (17cm)
Bulb spacing 4in (10cm)
Average height 1ft 8in (50cm)
Companion plants It's very pretty with the delicate foliage and flower heads of *Leucojum aestivum* (summer snowflake)
As a cut flower Excellent
Forcing No
Similar varieties 'Double Flaming Parrot' is the multi-petaled version, and 'Grand Perfection' has similar coloring and markings

Rococo

As ruffled and draped as a cinema curtain, 'Rococo' is a vibrant flounce of a flower. It buds green with purple flames, and as the bud breaks it reveals an intense damson-red interior with petals trimmed in scarlet. The bloom opens and flattens, displaying huge, feathered scarlet petals in shades of crimson, carmine and violet, while the exterior of the petal bears the bluer tones of raspberry, damson and violet. A sulfur-yellow basal blotch on each petal illuminates the heart of the flower, which houses a pale yellow pistil with a pale green cap ringed by inky-black stamens. As 'Rococo' boasts large flower heads, you are advised to plant it in a sheltered spot.

'Rococo' was registered by H. Slegtkamp & Co. in 1942. It took the Japan Bulb of the Year Award in 2003.

Type Parrot
Flowering Mid to late Spring
Aspect Full sun
Soil Fertile, well-drained soil
Planting depth 7in (17cm)
Bulb spacing 4in (10cm)
Average height 1ft 2in (35cm)
Companion plants Choose tulips that will complement the strong color palette of 'Rococo,' such as the dark purple of 'Queen of Night' and 'Black Parrot' or the dark red 'Uncle Tom'
As a cut flower Intense and attention-grabbing
Forcing No
Similar varieties 'Doorman's Record' is scarlet rather than crimson, and the tips of its petals are touched with yellow

Esperanto

This flamboyant but decidedly elegant tulip is a package of pure delight from start to finish. The green bud emerges from amid the stylish leaves, which are gray-green edged in white, then from the central green flame along the midrib creeps white, followed by hints of shell pink and rose. As the flower prepares to open the wavy-edged, pointy-tipped petals flood with color; shell pink bleeds into fuchsia, raspberry and scarlet, all echoing the shape of the green flame, each one like a Technicolor flaming torch. The moss-green flame also shifts hue, bleeding into damson at its outer reaches. The color combination is both bold and exquisite. Shaped like a squat flute, the petals expand to reveal a yellow-green heart with a sculptural cream pistil ringed by inky-black and old-gold stamens. This cultivar is perfect for planting in containers and with its petite stature also works well at the front of the flower bed.

'Esperanto' was registered in 1968 by J. Pranger. It was given the Royal Horticultural Society Award of Garden Merit in 1999.

Type Viridiflora
Flowering Late spring
Aspect Full sun
Soil Fertile, well-drained soil
Planting depth 7in (17cm)
Bulb spacing 4in (10cm)
Average height 12in (30cm)
Companion plants *Stachys byzantina* (lamb's ear)
As a cut flower Exceptional
Forcing No
Similar varieties 'Hollywood Star' is redder in color

Rems Favourite

In its color and markings this tulip is reminiscent of the Rembrandt tulips favored by the Dutch Masters, all indelibly marked by the mosaic virus. This remarkable bloom buds pale green and bursts open to reveal white petals finely etched with wine-red tongues of flame which lick the exterior and interior of each petal. In the heart of the flower the petals sport canary-yellow basal blotches that offset the green pistil, topped with a lemon cap, and the sulfur-yellow stamens. This is an elegant flower in both the flower bed and in a vase, where you can watch the flowers open and the petals drop in your own perfect still life.

'Rems Favourite' was introduced by Vertuco B.V. in 2000.

Type Triumph
Flowering Mid to late spring
Aspect Full sun
Soil Fertile, well-drained soil
Planting depth 7in (17cm)
Bulb spacing 4in (10cm)
Average height 1ft 10in (55cm)
Companion plants *Tulipa* 'Sarah Raven'
As a cut flower Stupendous – the stems wave and curl and the flower heads bow
Forcing Yes
Similar varieties 'Happy Generation' is white with scarlet feathering and is also in the Triumph group

Apricot Parrot

When it comes to tulips with names that fail to do them justice, this is the prime example. While apricot can indeed be seen on the petals, 'Apricot Parrot' is actually a heart-warming, dizzyingly flamboyant bloom that blends hot pink, orange and white to fabulous effect. This is the most painterly of blooms, deserving close examination.

'Apricot Parrot' buds a greeny-white, and as it breaks flashes of orange, old rose, mint, violet and lemon are revealed. The petals are fringed along the spine and curl back to reveal sudden flashes of color. As the bloom opens it transforms into a harmonious sunset of vivid brights; apricot and cream petals feathered in green unfurl and flatten to reveal a kaleidoscope of orange, apricot, sugar pink, coral, violet and yellow that glows in the sun. The pistil is green topped with a sculptural yellow cap and the stamens are long and inky-black.

On top of its flamboyant beauty, 'Apricot Parrot' is a good little performer in the flower bed, being sturdy and reliable. It was given the Royal Horticultural Society Award of Garden Merit in 1993. 'Apricot Parrot' was registered by H.G. Huyg in 1961.

Type Parrot
Flowering Mid to late spring
Aspect Full sun
Soil Fertile, well-drained soil
Planting depth 7in (17cm)
Bulb spacing 4in (10cm)
Average height 1ft 8in (50cm)
Companion plants Mix with dark tulips such as 'Queen of Night' or 'Black Parrot'
As a cut flower Spectacular flowers that warrant close examination
Forcing No
Similar varieties 'Rasta Parrot' is more emphatically orange in hue but it is similarly vibrant

Flaming Spring Green

This indisputably elegant and beautifully marked tulip buds green with white tips and opens to a delicately painted bloom. The ivory-white petals are licked with delicate flames of green and plum that extend across the petals as the bloom matures, turning shades of scarlet and moss green. The flower expands to form a perfect bowl shape. Peer into the exotic heart and you'll see that the lower half of each petal is washed lime green and the deep-red feathering appears in a near-perfect repeat pattern, so it looks like a subtly hued kaleidoscope. The green pistil is capped with a white tricorn, the anthers are yellow and the filaments dark violet. This tulip is particularly lovely when surrounded by green foliage.

'Flaming Spring Green' was introduced in 1999 by J. de Wit & Sons, bulb growers from the Netherlands.

Type Viridiflora
Flowering Late spring
Aspect Full sun
Soil Fertile, well-drained soil
Planting depth 6in (15cm)
Bulb spacing 4–6in (10–15cm)
Average height 1ft 4in–1ft 8in (40–50cm)
Companion plants *Euphorbia characias*
As a cut flower Indisputably stylish
Forcing No
Similar varieties 'Spring Green' – the same minus the red feathering

Doorman's Record

One could simply state that 'Doorman's Record' is a red tulip, but this does neither the bloom nor the color justice as there are so many shades of red. This tulip is an emphatic scarlet, a red with hints of orange that is the most joyful of colors. Its intensity is heightened by flames of brick and crimson, and tongues of moss green. Each petal has a delicate trim of sulfur yellow and is embellished with tiny pins of intense red that peel away from the petal. The flower buds a damson green with glimpses of coppery curls and unfurls into a bloom of a rich intensity. At the heart of the cupped bloom the petals have canary-yellow basal blotches that offset the pale pistil and inky-black stamens.

'Doorman's Record' was registered in 1975 by A. Bakkum and others.

Type Parrot
Flowering Mid spring
Aspect Full sun
Soil Fertile, well-drained soil
Planting depth 7in (17cm)
Bulb spacing 4in (10cm)
Average height 1ft 4in–1ft 8in (40–50cm)
Companion plants Celebrate its intense color by planting with dark purple tulips such as 'Queen of Night' or 'Black Parrot,' or coppery wallflowers (*Erysimum cheiri*)
As a cut flower Pure drama in a vase
Forcing No
Similar varieties 'Rococo'

THE WHIMSICAL DELIGHT

Artist

Appropriately for its name, 'Artist' is a painterly tulip that shifts through a wonderful color palette like a Turner painting. It buds a rich moss green, flecked with damson, and as the bloom unfurls it reveals splashes of dark purple, salmon pink, orange and hints of gold. The petals then turn a pale salmon pink, daubed with flames that flicker from green to plum, raspberry, violet, shell pink, butter and copper, each bleeding into the next in fine veins of pigment. This tulip is quite short, with wavy gray-green foliage. Mix it with rich and dark colors in the flower bed. It is a reliable performer and does equally well in both borders and containers.

'Artist' was registered by Captein Bros in 1947 and was given a Royal Horticultural Society Award of Garden Merit in 1995.

Type Viridiflora
Flowering Mid to late spring
Aspect Full sun
Soil Fertile, well-drained soil
Planting depth 7in (17cm)
Bulb spacing 4–6in (10–15cm)
Average height 12in (30cm)
Companion plants Wallflowers (*Erysimum*) in blood-red and rust
As a cut flower The rich bi-coloring allows it to blend beautifully in mixed bouquets
Forcing No
Similar varieties 'Green River' is a copper and green Viridiflora

Tulipa acuminata

This flamboyant and wiry eccentric is not a species tulip but a cultivar whose origins are unknown, although it was noted as growing in Copenhagen Botanic Gardens in 1813. Its correct name is variously held to be *T. cornuta* or *T.* 'Cornuta,' but you could look in vain for such a plant as bulb growers continue to refer to it and sell it as *T. acuminata*.

Budding green on slender stems, *T. acuminata* unfurls long, narrow, wayward yellow petals, edged in crimson, that twist and bend so that each resembles a flame. The pistil is green and topped by a jaunty yellow cap, while the stamens are yellow. The whole effect is individual, artful and eye-catching. The flower heads twist and arch prettily on their stems and stand proud from the foliage.

T. acuminata doesn't bloom for long, but it is well worth planting. It is favored by garden designers and the bulbs tend to sell out early in the buying season, so you'll need to be quick if you want to plant these beauties in your garden. It is also known under the common name of 'Fire Flame.'

Type Miscellaneous
Flowering Mid to late spring
Aspect Full sun or partial shade
Soil Fertile, well-drained soil
Planting depth 4in (10cm)
Bulb spacing 3in (7.5cm)
Average height 1ft 4in–1ft 8in (40–50cm)
Companion plants The low-growing *Tulipa tarda* or daylilies (*Hemerocallis*)
As a cut flower A talking point
Forcing No
Similar varieties One of a kind

Carnaval de Nice

Looking more like a peony than a tulip, 'Carnaval de Nice' is a ravishing meringue of a bloom that is a perfect fit in a cottage-garden border. It buds green and bursts open to reveal densely packed white petals splashed with abstract streaks of crimson. Look harder and you'll find tiny splashes of yellow, green and violet. As the bloom expands the petals can become infused with a pale pink flush and the red streaks dilute to feathers of raspberry pink. Despite making something of a statement, the soft color palette of 'Carnaval de Nice' means it blends beautifully with many plants in the border. At the heart of the flower the petals carry a yellow basal blotch that illuminates the pale green pistil and inky-black stamens. The blousy flower heads stand proud of the gray-green foliage, tipped in white.

'Carnaval de Nice' was introduced in 1953 by C.G. van Tubergen, a bulb nursery established in the Netherlands in 1868. It was given the Royal Horticultural Society Award of Garden Merit in 1999.

Type Double Late
Flowering Late spring
Aspect Full sun
Soil Fertile, well-drained soil
Planting depth 6in (15cm)
Bulb spacing 4in (10cm)
Average height 1ft 8in (50cm)
Companion plants Plant with bushy herbaceous geraniums or white *Narcissus*
As a cut flower A sumptuous marvel
Forcing No
Similar varieties 'Flaming Margarita'

Tulipa didieri

This charming species tulip hails from Savoy in France, where it once grew wild in the Western Alps. It is described as a neo-tulipae – a species that was originally brought from Asia and then became naturalized in Europe. *T. didieri* produces elegant blooms with deep red, pointed, lily-like petals that curl back, revealing a black basal blotch topped with a narrow cream trim, each hue bleeding harmoniously into its neighbor.

This tulip buds green tipped with red, the color intensifying as the bloom matures and unfurls, acquiring a glossy sheen. The stamens are a deep, dark violet and the pistil a creamy yellow. Like many species tulips, it can be variable and sometimes bears yellow or white flowers. It produces just three or four leaves, which grow tall and narrowly pointed.

Type Species
Flowering Mid to late spring
Aspect Full sun
Soil Fertile, well-drained soil
Planting depth 3in (7.5cm)
Bulb spacing 2in (5cm)
Average height 12in (30cm)
Companion plants Plant it with a mass of *Puschkinia*, a pretty white and blue flower that blooms a little earlier but also enjoys a dry summer
As a cut flower Enjoy *in situ*. Pick to your heart's content once the tulip has spread and naturalized
Forcing No
Similar varieties *Tulipa systola*, although this is best grown in pots and left unwatered in a greenhouse over the summer

Tulipa aucheriana

The flowers of this shy tulip peep out in bunches on short stems from the base of its generously proportioned tangle of leaves. The long pink buds open into starry little flowers that fully revert in the sun. The white-tipped, rose-pink petals have a yellow-brown basal blotch edged in white; this in turn bleeds into the pink. The pistil is pale green topped with a yellow cap and the stamens are yellow. It hails from Iran and was introduced in 1880 by Henry Elwes, an avid collector of lilies and butterflies. It was named in honor of the elaborately named French plant collector Pierre Martin Rémi Aucher-Éloy, who had earlier collected this specimen.

Plant in a sunny situation with good drainage – troughs are ideal – and leave it to its own devices to happily naturalize and spread. It was given the Royal horticultural Society Award of Garden Merit in 1993.

Type Miscellaneous
Flowering Mid spring
Aspect Full sun
Soil Fertile, well-drained soil
Planting depth 3in (7.5cm)
Bulb spacing 3in (7.5cm)
Average height 4–6in (10–15cm)
Companion plants Mix with other alpines in a trough
As a cut flower Too small and pretty to pick
Forcing No
Similar varieties *T. humilis* 'Odalisque'

Lady Jane

Diminutive 'Lady Jane' is a chameleon in character, although she will take a little time to settle in. The long, pinky-green buds stand erect on wiry stems and mature to reveal delicate flute flowers that fully revert in the sun to form exquisite star-shaped blooms. The wonder of 'Lady Jane' is that the reverses of three petals are a warm rose pink edged in white that tightly enclose three white petals, but when fully open, all the inner petals are white with the faintest pink blush, so first you have a pink flower and then you have a white one. At the heart of the flower is a yellow basal blotch, which frames the green, lemon-tipped pistil and long inky-black stamens. The leaves are thin and arching and great clumps can establish over time. Once settled into position, 'Lady Jane' will spread and multiply via underground stolons and when the sun shines will provide a veritable carpet of starry white flowers.

A cultivated form of *Tulipa clusiana*, 'Lady Jane' was registered by W. van Lierop & Zn. B.V. in 1992. These forms of cultivated species tulips are commonly dubbed "botanical tulips." 'Lady Jane' was given the Royal Horticultural Society Award of Garden Merit in 2008.

Type Miscellaneous
Flowering Early spring
Aspect Full sun
Soil Fertile, well-drained soil
Planting depth 4in (10cm)
Bulb spacing 3in (7.5cm)
Average height 10in (25cm)
Companion plants *Anemone blanda*
As a cut flower Sweetly pretty
Forcing No
Similar varieties *T. clusiana* 'Peppermint Stick'

Oviedo

This delicately colored tulip appears to be pink at first glance, but closer inspection reveals a complex coloration. 'Oviedo' buds pale green and unfurls to reveal a white tulip shaded through with finely sketched plum-colored lines in varying degrees of intensity, so that it shifts in hue from blue-white through lavender and into dark plum patches of shadowing. The inner petals are palest lavender, etched with yellow at the base. The petals are lightly topped with wayward fringing.

'Oviedo' was registered in 2008 by Vertuco B.V., a Dutch company that specializes in the cultivation and distribution of tulips.

Type Fringed
Flowering Mid to late spring
Aspect Full sun
Soil Fertile, well-drained soil
Planting depth 6–8in (15–20cm)
Bulb spacing 4in (10cm)
Average height 1ft 4in–1ft 8in (40–50cm)
Companion plants *Myosotis alpestris* 'White' (forget-me-not)
As a cut flower Charming
Forcing No
Similar varieties 'Blue Heron' is a Fringed tulip with a soft violet color

GREEN MILE [above], FANCY FRILLS [right]

Tulipa clusiana var. chrysantha

Delicate in appearance but deceptively tough, this little tulip will happily reproduce and spread if it is in the right position. It buds green on drooping stems, but, as these straighten and turn purple, the bud stands erect. Three outer petals are Indian red and as these open three canary-yellow inner-petals, stained red at the base are revealed. The petals are long, slender and beautifully shaped to a pointed tip, curving to form an elegant flute. On cloudy days the flower remains closed, but in sunshine it opens fully to reveal a starry yellow interior, with a pale green pistil and yellow stamens. The long, slender, gray-green leaves droop prettily in elegant arches, so the flower heads stand well above the foliage. Hailing from the Caucasus, it thrives in well-drained soil, but appreciates shelter from wind and excessive rain. It will also work well as a container plant.

T. clusiana var. *chrysantha* was given the Royal Horticultural Society Award of Garden Merit in 1993. Named after Carolus Clusius, the 16th-century Dutch botanist, it is also known as the golden lady tulip.

Type Miscellaneous
Flowering Mid spring
Aspect Full sun
Soil Fertile, well-drained soil
Planting depth 6in (15cm)
Bulb spacing 4in (10cm)
Average height 8in (20cm)
Companion plants Give it space to spread and shine alone
As a cut flower Delicate and distinctive
Forcing Yes
Similar varieties The reverse of the three outer petals of *T. kolpakowskiana* are rusty orange rather than red

Tulipa linifolia

T. linifolia may be small, but it cuts quite a dash in the flower bed with its gleaming, highly polished petals and vivid scarlet hue. It buds green then opens to reveal very large, beautifully cut petals with pointed tips that open out and revert to form a shallow bowl. Each petal has a purple-black basal blotch and this rings the pale green pistil, topped pale yellow. The long stamens stand out like fake eyelashes, almost too long, thick, and purple-black to be real, although the species is variable, and it can produce yellow stamens. The foliage is slender and wavy-edged with a central rib and splays out in a whorl.

It hails from Iran and Central Asia and, if planted in a suitably well-drained, sunny and sheltered spot, this species tulip will naturalize and flower year after year. *T. linifolia* was given the Royal Horticultural Society Award of Garden Merit in 1993.

Type Species
Flowering Mid to late spring
Aspect Full sun
Soil Fertile, well-drained soil
Planting depth 4–6in (10–15cm)
Bulb spacing 3in (7.5cm)
Average height 4in (10cm)
Companion plants Let it shine alone in the flower bed
As a cut flower Because the stems are short, enjoy it *in situ*
Forcing No
Similar varieties *T. batalinii* is the same in form, but soft yellow in color

Claudia

'Claudia' is a neat, elegant bloom that cuts quite a dash in the flower bed. Its purity of shape is highlighted by the intense raspberry-pink petals that bleed into a trim of white. The bases of the petals are white and encircle a green, yellow-capped pistil ringed by violet filaments topped by yellow anthers. The green bud breaks revealing hints of pink, then opens further into an upright pink curl of petals with chinks of white showing through. It acquires a trim waist before maturing into a perfectly elegant cup of fluted petals. The bloom stands proud of the foliage and the long slender stems are prone to wind damage, so plant it in a sheltered spot.

'Claudia' was introduced in 1998 by J.W. Reus Bloembollen B.V., a tulip nursery in the Netherlands.

Type Lily-flowered
Flowering Mid to late spring
Aspect Full sun
Soil Fertile, well-drained soil
Planting depth 6–8in (15–20cm)
Bulb spacing 4–6in (10–15cm)
Average height 2ft (60cm)
Companion plants Stunning with *Tulipa* 'Queen of Night' or *T.* 'White Triumphator' and *Lamprocapnos spectabilis* 'Alba' (white bleeding heart)
As a cut flower Excellent solo or mixed with other white and pink flowers
Forcing Yes
Similar varieties 'Ballade' is almost identical at a quick glance, but the petals fully revert in maturity

West Point

'West Point' is a tulip with military bearing, standing firmly upright on tall stems. The exquisite, Lily-flowered blooms are held erect – no slouching here – head and shoulders above the gray-green, wavy-edged foliage. However, this noble stance can cause it to suffer from wind damage, so it performs best in a sheltered spot. The green buds open to a green-tinged yellow, but as it matures from a tight bud the tone warms and loses its acidic hue. The petals of the fluted flowers revert in a neat fold and are long and tapering, twisting prettily with age. Peer inside and you'll find a green pistil ringed by yellow stamens; take the opportunity to breathe in its sweet fragrance. A large clump will sway elegantly with the breeze like a well-drilled dance troupe.

'West Point' was registered in 1943 by De Mol & A.H. Nieuwenhuis.

Type Lily-flowered
Flowering Late spring
Aspect Full sun
Soil Fertile, well-drained soil
Planting depth 7in (17cm)
Bulb spacing 4in (10cm)
Average height 1ft 8in (50cm)
Companion plants Dot the bulbs haphazardly around clumps of daylilies such as the yellow Spider *Hemerocallis* 'Chester Cyclone,' or the plum-colored *H.* 'Buckyballs'
As a cut flower Striking
Forcing No
Similar varieties 'Budlight' is a white and yellow Lily-flowered tulip

Queensland

'Queensland' is the cotton candy of the tulip world; a saccharine feast of over-the-top, girlish-pink femininity, topped by ruffled frills. It is quite a sight in full bloom and deserves to be celebrated. Budding green, as the double bloom begins to unfurl its petals are grass green flushed with salmon-pink flames before turning rosy-pink. The tattered petal edges unfurl into pale pink fringing. The color continues to fade as the flower matures into a frilly, pale pink confection, though it remains raspberry pink near the heart so that the overall effect is a rippling pink ice-cream sundae. At the center lies a pale willow-green pistil ringed with buttery-yellow stamens. The foliage is standard tulip fare, topped with this marvelous tutu of a bloom.

'Queensland' was registered by Vertuco B.V. in 2006.

Type Fringed
Flowering Mid to late spring
Aspect Full sun
Soil Fertile, well-drained soil
Planting depth 8in (20cm)
Bulb spacing 4in (10cm)
Average height 12in (30cm)
Companion plants *Myosotis* (forget-me-not) in blue, pink or white, or a mix of all three
As a cut flower Very pretty
Forcing No
Similar varieties 'Bell Song' is another Fringed pink variety, but a tad less girlish in hue

Doll's Minuet

Tall for a Viridiflora, 'Doll's Minuet' produces fat green buds streaked in white. As the bud matures and starts to break it reveals a cherry-red flower with minute dashes of violet, streaked with willow green and moss green feathering along the central rib. As the bloom opens, the feathering turns from green to damson to dark violet and the pointy-tipped petals form a neat, upturned bell shape. The petals do not fully revert, but as the bloom ages they lengthen and twist as though reaching and stretching. 'Doll's Minuet' has a very starchy, upright posture but will bow to the pressure of the rain and then regain its original stance when dry. It will produce flowers for more than one season if left *in situ*, although the display will be weaker the following year.

As 'Doll's Minuet' is a strong bluish-pink in tone, take care where you place it in relation to the other garden plants. It works well with green, dark purples and blues, performing well in containers as well as the border.

'Doll's Minuet' was registered in 1968 by the Dutch bulb growers Konijnenburg & Mark.

Type Viridiflora
Flowering Late spring
Aspect Full sun
Soil Fertile, well-drained soil
Planting depth 7in (17cm)
Bulb spacing 4in (10cm)
Average height 1ft 2in (35cm)
Companion plants If in doubt opt for *Muscari* (grape hyacinth) or *Myosotis* (forget-me-not)
As a cut flower Vibrant
Forcing No
Similar varieties 'Purple Doll,' as its name suggests, is violet and purple, with green flames

Bastia

Part of the delight of this tulip is that within a rich color spectrum of plum, copper and yellow ocher you never quite know what you are going to get. Budding a green flecked with purple, as the bloom unfurls it reveals the purple petals edged in rusty-orange. As the flower matures and opens the colors can become lighter and richer, with plum stripes and a fringe of yellow ocher, although its petals conceal the green pistil and inky-black stamens. The double blooms are fulsome and, with the lavish fringe embellishment and dramatic coloring, they are reminiscent of opulent swagged and trimmed 1930s lampshades. This is an absolute showstopper in the border.

Bastia was registered in 2011 by Vertuco B.V. in the Netherlands.

Type Fringed
Flowering Mid to late spring
Aspect Full sun
Soil Fertile, well-drained soil
Planting depth 10–15cm
Bulb spacing 4–6in (10–15cm)
Companion plants Mix with wallflowers (*Erysimum*) in blood-red and rust
Average height 1ft 4in (40cm)
As a cut flower Rich and exotic
Forcing No
Similar varieties One of a kind

Virichic

Budding green, 'Virichic' opens into a beautifully shaped, lily-like tulip with a wonderful fluted shape. The color evolves as the bloom matures. Rippling pale pink petals initially bear a leaf-green flame that runs from pointed tip to base; the colors intensify after a few days, the pale pink deepens to a vibrant sugar pink and the flame shrinks to a single moss-green spine with a flickering pale yellow shadow. The green pistil is topped by a lemon cap and the filaments are maroon with yellow anthers. As the flower heads move in the breeze, the green flames blend with the surrounding foliage so that the whole display is a shimmering, mobile visual feast.

'Virichic' was registered in 2002 by Holland Bolroy Markt B.V., a Dutch company that specializes in the introduction of new bulbs to the market.

Type Viridiflora
Flowering Late spring
Aspect Full sun
Soil Fertile, well-drained soil
Planting depth 7in (17cm)
Bulb spacing 4in (10cm)
Average height 1ft 8in (50cm)
Companion plants *Camassia leichtlinii*
As a cut flower A real beauty that blends well with other pink flowers
Forcing No
Similar varieties 'China Town'

Shirley

There is something reminiscent of a sweet pea in the delicate color palette and patterning of this tall tulip. It buds a creamy-green and opens ivory-white, each petal bordered with the finest vein of lavender, from which a series of finely etched lines and dots radiate outwards. The petals, which look almost translucent, form a lovely cupped shape. As the flower matures the delicate lavender shading spreads around the petals, intensifying the color, but the delight is that each petal and each bloom are slightly different. Gaze into the heart of this flower and you'll see that the petals are shaded a rich blue, the pistil is a cream flourish and it is ringed by inky-black stamens. Despite its delicate appearance as a member of the Triumph family, this is a very robust tulip.

'Shirley' was hybridized by Mr F.C. Bik, a former pilot from Schoorl in the Netherlands, and registered in 1968 by Jacques Tol Junior, a tulip breeder and hybridizer from Sint Pancras. Jacques and his colleague Mr F.C. Bik are best known for breeding 'Pinocchio,' a diminutive red and white bloom that happily naturalizes.

Type Triumph
Flowering Mid to late spring
Aspect Full sun
Soil Fertile, well-drained soil
Planting depth 7in (17cm)
Bulb spacing 4in (10cm)
Average height 1ft 6in–1ft 8in (45–50cm)
Companion plants *Myosotis alpestris* 'White' (forget-me-not), *Nigella damascena* (love-in-a-mist) or *Tulipa* 'Negrita'
As a cut flower Soft and delicate, equally pretty in white and cream arrangements
Forcing Yes
Similar varieties 'Infinity'

Tulipa whittallii

Hailing from Turkey, this charming tulip produces neat rust-colored blooms that stand erect on slender stems. It buds yellow-green and opens to reveal a small goblet-shaped flower. Each petal is precisely marked with a dark basal blotch, ringed with a yellow flare and divided by a fine central stripe. The pistil is yellow-green tipped, topped with a yellow-orange cap, and the dark green filaments have inky-black anthers. In the right surroundings this tulip will happily spread.

Edward Whittall (1851–1917) was a keen botanist who created a beautiful garden packed with native plants in Bornova, Turkey, where his family ran a fig and currant export business. Here he entertained such luminaries as the Prince of Wales, later King George V, and the writer Gertrude Bell. Whittall identified seven new plant species and these were named *whittallii* in recognition. Other plants including a snowdrop and a *Fritillaria* bear his name. There is some disagreement amongst botanists as to whether *T. whittallii* is actually a variant of *T. orphanidea* and it is now commonly listed as *T. orphanidea* Whittallii Group. This species was photographed in the Cambridge Botanic Garden where it is labeled as *T. whittallii* and we have listed it accordingly.

Type Miscellaneous
Flowering Mid to late spring
Aspect Full sun
Soil Fertile, well-drained soil
Planting depth 8in (20cm)
Bulb spacing 3in (7.5cm)
Average height 10in (25cm)
Companion plants Use *Fritillaria uva-vulpis* as a backdrop and *Iris tuberosa* in the foreground
As a cut flower Very pretty
Forcing Yes
Similar varieties *T. orphanidea* 'Flava' has yellow petals with orange-red tips

GROWING AND CARE

CENTURIES OF CULTIVATION HAVE RESULTED IN TULIPS IN A GLORIOUS DIVERSITY OF FORMS, COLORS AND MARKINGS. YOU WILL FIND IT EASY TO BRING THEIR BEAUTY INTO YOUR GARDEN AS LONG AS YOU FOLLOW THE BASIC RULES.

The life cycle of a bulb

A bulb is a food-storage organ which nurtures a plant during winter. Unlike other species of bulbs, such as daffodils or hyacinths, a mature tulip bulb blooms only once. It uses its energy reserves to shoot and grow leaves and flowers and also to produce new offset bulbs, a process that continues even as the leaves and stems die back. The mother bulb then withers and dies. Some tulip cultivars are more efficient in the production and strength of the next generation in the form of offsets than others. They will continue to flower for a few years when left *in situ*, albeit less impressively with each passing year.

The thin, papery outer layers of the bulb – the tunic – protect the interior. Inside are fleshy leaves called scales which encircle the stem, an immature flower bud, and a basal stem which connects the flower bud, the leaf scales and the compressed stem to the roots. The roots grow from this basal stem. Lateral bulbs, or offsets, begin to grow just above the basal stem. If you cut the bulb in half from top to bottom you can easily see these parts in the cross-section – a waste of a bulb, but a fascinating exercise.

After planting, a tulip bulb begins to grow a root system that enables it to take up water and nutrients and to establish a firm base to support and anchor the plant when it produces leaves and flowers. As the temperatures drop, the bulb undergoes a rest period; it needs 10–16 weeks of cold weather where temperatures drop to a minimum of at least 41°F (5°C), although it can withstand much colder conditions. As temperatures rise, the bulb begins to convert its store of starches into sugar and the leaves and embryo flower begin to grow and push up and out of the bulb.

Once the bulb has bloomed, it is very important that tulip cultivars are deadheaded so that the plant does not waste energy on seed production. However, they must be allowed to die back naturally, as the leaves and stem continue to provide nutrients for the burgeoning offsets. The bulb then enters a period of dormancy.

Climate control

As tulips hail from Central Asia and south-eastern Europe roughly along the latitude of 40°N, they survive very cold winters with the bulbs safely tucked up under a blanket of snow in an insulating bed of earth. They enjoy hot, dry summers basking in the sun, require plenty of water in the spring growing season, and like a good circulation of air, preferably in a sheltered spot where their leggy stems are not blasted by strong winds.

The majority of the world's tulip bulbs are cultivated in the Netherlands, which does not have the ideal climate. However, growers subject their bulbs to heat and humidity treatments to replicate their natural environment, so that when buyers receive them in the autumn they are primed and ready to be tucked up in a cool bed for winter.

The US Department of Agriculture (USDA) climatic areas are divided into numeric zones which range from Zone 1 in areas such as Anchorage, Alaska to Zone 12 in Hawaii. Tulips can be planted in hardiness Zones 3–10, but planting times will need to be adjusted accordingly. Residents of Zones 3–5 should plant bulbs in September and October, Zones 6–7 in October and November, Zones 8–9 in November and December and Zone 10 December and January.

If you live in a warmer climate, such as USDA Zone 8–10, you will need to replicate a period of cold to trigger root growth, as is done when tulips are "forced" to bloom early. This is easily achieved by chilling bulbs in a refrigerator for 8–10 weeks prior to the recommended planting date for your zone. For more information on chilling tulip bulbs, see Forcing, p.218.

The perfect bed

Plant tulips in a sunny spot; in the northern hemisphere a south or south-west-facing border will produce the best results, and they will grow straight of stem. They don't appreciate being cast into the shade of walls, fences, hedges or other plants, although some cultivars are more tolerant of partial shade. Remember that many shrubs and trees will not be in leaf when tulips are actively growing, so spots that are shady in summer may provide sufficient sunshine in spring. Steer clear of frost pockets, where buds and young leaves may be damaged, and damp, boggy spots.

Tulips require a well-drained soil; if planted in heavy, wet soil, the bulbs are inclined to rot and fall prey to diseases. Soil is graded according to its clay, silt and sand content. The size and proportion of these mineral particles affect the behavior of the soil. Loam soils have the perfect combination of mineral particles, with about 10–25 percent clay – a mix that offers high fertility with good drainage and water retention. All soils can be improved with compost and well-matured cow (not horse) manure.

The ideal soil for growing tulips is neutral to slightly alkaline, with a pH level of 6–7. Soil pH testing kits, readily available in shops and garden centers, will inform you of the pH of your own soil. A pH of 7 indicates a neutral soil, while a reading above 7 will indicate an alkaline one. It is possible to slightly raise or lower the pH levels – adding sulfur or lime to the soil makes it more acid or alkaline respectively.

If drainage is poor, or the soil is heavy clay, mix in some gravel or coarse grit. You can also add sharp sand to the bottom of the hole before planting to further aid drainage. Tulips do need moisture, especially in the growing season, so if you have a sandy soil add some leaf mold (well-rotted leaves) and compost. Dig the area over to a depth of 10in (25cm) while you are incorporating the organic matter.

Drainage aside, tulips are quite tolerant, but any effort you put into improving the soil will reap handsome rewards in the strength and vigor of the resulting plants and their ongoing ability to produce healthy offsets.

PARROT NEGRITA [above], SYNAEDA BLUE [right]   214

Planting tulips in the garden

Plant tulips in late autumn or early winter. Dig a hole in a sunny spot and incorporate some organic matter; if drainage is poor add gravel or coarse grit. The bulbs should sit on a thin layer of sharp sand, approximately 6–7in/15–17cm below the surface. Space them at about 6in (15cm) intervals. Backfill with soil.

Planting

Tulips are tough bulbs, hailing from regions where the winters are very cold indeed, and they require a period of chilling in the ground where the temperature outdoors drops to at least 41°F (5°C) in order to promote growth and flowering. Tulips grow easily in the temperate climate that prevails in most of Europe, but if your climate is warmer you will have to help the bulbs along with a period of artificial chilling (see Forcing, p.218). You will also find that bulbs struggle to reproduce naturally if spring is very warm, so bulbs are likely to be good for only one season.

In temperate zones tulips can be planted from mid-autumn to early winter, which is a little later than most spring-flowering bulbs. Do not be tempted to plant tulip bulbs as soon as an early order arrives. Store the bulbs somewhere cool and dry, out of direct light, and wait for the prescribed time. It is cold that triggers the bulb's growth, so if it is planted early it will simply sit in damp soil and be susceptible to rot. If you can wait until late autumn, or even early winter, the bulbs will be less susceptible to disease and the emerging foliage will be less likely to suffer from frost damage in the spring.

PLANTING IN THE BORDER

As a general rule, bulbs are planted in groups of five, nine, eleven and so on, in a drift. It is more aesthetically pleasing to plant an odd number, which creates a relaxed and natural feel. Tulips can thus be used to fill gaps in the border. When ordering, bear in mind what will be growing behind and in front of them, as well as the time they put on growth and come into bloom. Ideally the tulip flowers will rise elegantly above their neighbors rather than being semi-concealed by them. Consider planting cultivars of slightly different heights and flower sizes in clumps near each other to enhance the easy, relaxed feel.

As a simple rule of thumb, tulips should be planted at a depth that is three times the height of the bulb – bulb size varies according to class and cultivar. However, planting them

each consecutive line so that the tulips in the second row sit neatly behind the gaps in the front row. The third row echoes the first row, and so on.

If your garden is small you can dot tulips in clumps where there are gaps in the planting, and when they have died down and been lifted you can put late summer-flowering plants such as dahlias in their place.

COMPANION PLANTING

It is the company you choose for your tulips that will set the mood of the planting. I prefer tulips to be slightly screened fore and aft by other plants so that the eye does not focus on their leggy upright form, but rather on their swaying blooms floating above a sea of foliage and other flowers. Herbaceous perennials such as geraniums, peonies, poppies (*Papaver*) and daylilies (*Hemerocallis*) can work as a low screen for tulips, and if they flower later than your particular cultivars you only need to consider if the shade of their foliage is compatible.

There are tried and tested favorites; forget-me-nots (*Myosotis*) and wallflowers (*Erysimum*) are perfect bedfellows. Plants bought from nurseries often turn out to include more than one color, so it is advisable to grow your own from seed to guarantee the production of a single color that will blend with your tulips for a harmonious drift. This is especially pertinent when planting very pale or strongly colored tulips. Reds can be hard to accommodate in the flower bed, but planting them among the foliage of herbaceous perennials that bloom later is a good way to avoid violent color clashes. Enjoy playing with different combinations of companion plants – you will quickly learn what works in your particular space, and what doesn't.

a little deeper, at 6–8in (15–20cm), gives further protection against penetrating frost and is advised in very cold regions. In milder areas with light frosts, planting the bulbs at 4–6in (10–15cm) will suffice. If in doubt plant deeper, as this provides the best protection against fluctuating temperatures.

To plant informally in meandering drifts, space bulbs at a minimum of 4–5in (10–13cm) apart, extending the spacing randomly. Dotting bulbs further apart here and there replicates the effect of self-seeding. This planting principle produces spectacular results and works beautifully in any garden.

Formal bedding, as seen in parks where serried lines of tulips stand to attention beside neat rows of pansies or wallflowers, exudes a certain grandeur when meticulously executed. Bulbs should be similarly spaced, at a distance of 4–5in (10–13cm), but planted in straight lines. If you are attempting such a precise planting, measure the distance and calculate how many bulbs will be required to plant each line of tulips. Stagger the spacing of

PLANTING IN A CONTAINER

Siting your tulips in containers is a great way of introducing spring color to the garden. When they are coming into flower, you can dot the pots here and there in the border to give the illusion of a perfectly planned scheme. When the tulips have bloomed they can be lifted and replaced with summer-flowering plants.

Tulips require deep containers with a diameter of at least 12in (30cm) so that the roots have room to grow. Check the height the tulips will reach and pick your container accordingly. Put crocks in the base to improve drainage and add around 4in (10cm) of bulb-planting compost or a loam-based soil with sand or grit mixed in. At this point add a fine layer of sharp sand to help keep the bases of the bulbs dry and thus avoid rot. Place the tulips centrally – in containers the usual rules of spacing do not apply and the bulbs can be placed close to each other, but not actually touching. Cover the bulbs with more compost until all you can see is the tips.

Encircle them with smaller spring-flowering bulbs, such as grape hyacinth (*Muscari*). These don't have to flower at the same time – you can choose them to extend the period of interest. Cover this underplanting with compost and fill the pot to within ½in (1cm) of the top, then water thoroughly just once. If an extended period without rain occurs and the soil becomes very dry, give the pot a soaking in a large container so it can take up the water naturally. Should you have a problem with squirrels or other pests digging up the bulbs or nibbling on them, cover the pots with chicken wire to deter them.

If you intend to lift the tulips for use the following year, feed them when they are

Planting tulips in a container

Use a pot that has a minimum depth of 12in (30cm). Place broken pieces of old flowerpot in the bottom of a large container to help drainage.

Add 4in (10cm) of bulb-planting compost or a loam-based soil with grit incorporated. Add a thin layer of sharp sand to keep the bases of the bulbs dry.

Space bulbs at intervals around the pot; you can plant them more closely than you would in the flowerbed. Backfill the pot with compost to within ½in (1cm) of the top.

If you are incorporating other bulbs within your planting, these should be layered to the correct depth. Smaller bulbs such as iris, crocus and muscari need to be planted closer to the surface than tulips, about 2in (5cm) deep.

throwing up leaves and forming buds so that they also have the energy to produce offsets. Otherwise discard the bulbs after flowering – they won't bloom again if you just plant them in the flower bed.

Species tulips require conditions that replicate their natural environment, namely cold winters, wet springs and dry summers. It is easier to reproduce these in a container – most struggle in a mixed border. They require deep containers of at least 8in (20cm) filled with good, gritty soil, topped with a mulch of grit or gravel. Here they can remain year in, year out, spreading and multiplying. There is no watering involved – indeed you will need to shelter them from rain in the summer. Feed them occasionally and repot the plants every few years.

Deadheading

Snip flower heads off tulip cultivars as soon as they die. If they are left *in situ* the continued development of the seed uses energy the plant could be putting towards the production of offsets, which is the only means of reliable propagation. Species tulips can be left to seed and will spread by seed and "droppers" (offsets that grow a short distance below the mother bulb).

Maintenance feeding

If you incorporated organic material to the soil prior to planting you do not need to give tulips any additional feed. However, if you want to give them a boost, apply a balanced general fertilizer in the spring. Avoid high-nitrogen fertilizers which promote leafy growth – you want one that is rich in potassium, or potash,

which promotes flowering, fruiting and vigor. Avoid the leaves when applying fertilizer as it can burn them.

If you intend to lift the tulips for use the following year, apply the same kind of fertilizer weekly when flowering has finished until the leaves die back. This will promote the development of offsets.

Lifting

You can simply leave tulips in the ground to see if they will flower the following year; some cultivars do this more efficiently than others. However, the chances are that your next spring show will be considerably diminished and quite probably it will be absent altogether. Lifting allows you to remove the offsets and to establish which ones may flower the following year, and which need to be placed in a nursery bed to mature further.

Lift bulbs with a spade just before the foliage completely disappears, but not any earlier, as the offsets will still be drawing nutrients from the leaves as they die back. Brush the soil away, then leave the bulbs somewhere cool and dry with what is left of the foliage. When this is completely dry you can twist it off and examine the bulbs.

Twist the offsets gently away from the mother bulb, which can be discarded. Store them in nets or paper bags out of sunlight and in a well-ventilated spot, ideally at a temperature of around 65–68°F (18–20°C). Check over the offsets before replanting. Discard any that are soft or spotted, and if you see any signs of aphids treat them with an insecticide. Inspect for size and any signs of damage; only plump, healthy offsets are worth propagating. The largest offsets may flower the following year, while smaller offsets

will take two or three years before they are ready to bloom. Plant small offsets in sunny, well-drained nursery beds 6in (15cm) deep and spaced at 6in (15cm) intervals to mature. In the growing season they will produce leaves that will feed the growing bulbs until they are sufficiently mature to flower, when the whole process begins again.

Tulip bulbs come in a range of shapes and sizes depending on the cultivar and group; you will learn by experience how long it will take the offsets of different cultivars to reach maturity. If you don't want to bother with nursery beds for the smaller offsets, simply use the largest daughter offset and discard the rest.

Forcing

Forcing is the process of tricking a bulb into responding to what seems to have been winter by starting to shoot and flower. Some groups and cultivars perform better than others. In theory most of the Groups 1–11 (see pp.12–14) are suitable, but for best results look out for cultivars that are said to be good for forcing. Some are better for very early forcing, which is why you may see so many bulbs of the same variety of tulip for sale in early spring.

To force tulip bulbs, put them in paper bags and place in the refrigerator at 34–41°F (1–5°C); the salad drawer, or crisper, is perfect. Do not store any fruit at the same time as these emit ethylene which will hinder the tulips' development. When the bulbs begin to sprout they are ready to pot (see p.218).

Put the pots out of direct sunlight in a room with a temperature of around 50–62°F (10–16.5°C) for two weeks. If possible keep the room cooler and darker initially, gradually adjusting light levels and temperatures so that

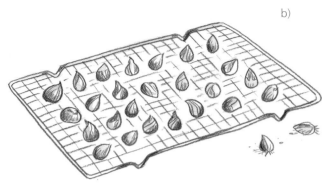

a)

b)

c)

Lifting and propagating

a) Remove flower heads as they fade to prevent the tulips using energy to set seed. Allow the tulip leaves to wither and die back, which sends nutrients back to the bulbs, before lifting each bulb gently. Remove the leaves and stalk; either twist them off by hand or use secateurs if you need to. Gently remove the offsets from the mother bulb, which can then be discarded.

b) Place the offsets on a tray to dry. Only the largest offsets will flower the following year. Smaller offsets can either be discarded or planted in nursery beds until they are large enough to flower.

c) Store the offsets in a string or paper bag away from direct sunlight, in a well-ventilated spot.

the plants can acclimatize. When the shoots are 2in (5cm) in height, move the pots to a bright, warm room, out of direct sunlight. The plants will rapidly grow, bud and come into flower in around a week.

This same process of simulating winter conditions can be used to cultivate tulips if you live in warm climates such as USDA Zones 8–10. Once the bulbs have been chilled they can be planted in the garden at the time of year when your soil is coolest. In Zones 8–9

this is in late November and early December, and in Zone 10 early January.

You can also force tulips to flower a little earlier by potting them up and storing them in a shed or unheated garage, or a refrigerator if you have one to spare with enough space for flowerpots. Soak the pot in a bowl of water so it can take up moisture gently, remove and cover with newspaper to keep the bulbs in darkness. Check them after about ten weeks, and as soon as the shoots emerge from the surface, follow the same procedure as above.

If tulip bulbs have been forced for indoor use there is little point in planting them in the garden afterwards, as it is very rare for them to flower again.

Pests and diseases

If you employ good husbandry tulips are relatively problem-free, especially in their first year. However, problems can sometimes occur; check any symptoms against the list below to find out how to address them.

EELWORM

These small thread-like organisms are barely visible to the naked eye. They feed on the bulb's root hairs in the soil then invade the plant, destroying the tissue from within. When the plant dies the eelworms move on to its neighbors. If you see bent stems and splitting leaves eelworms are present. Dig up any affected bulbs and burn them.

ROOT AND STEM ROT

This soil-borne fungal disease is very damaging, causing the leaves and shoots to wilt and turn brown. Dig up the plant and burn it. Tidy up the area and remove leaf debris. If you have been watering from a stored water supply, use a commercial eco-friendly liquid treatment product that is specifically designed to improve the quality of the water in the barrel. Emptying and cleaning the water barrel annually will help to avoid this problem.

SLUGS AND SNAILS

These pests will feed on both the foliage and the bulb below ground. Plant tulips in clean containers in fresh bulb compost and attempt to control the local population.

SQUIRRELS AND MICE

Squirrels will dig up tulip bulbs and mice will nibble at them. If this is a problem in your garden, cover the area or container with chicken wire to discourage them. The shoots will grow through it.

TULIP FIRE

Tulip fire (*Botrytis tulipae*) is the most common disease to affect tulips and once it appears it can spread rapidly among the plants. Tulips are most susceptible if the ground is too wet – hence the importance of establishing good drainage – and the atmosphere damp. The symptoms will appear on the foliage and stem, which will become spotted and distorted. As soon as you see these symptoms lift the bulb, complete with foliage, and burn it. Spray any other tulips with a systemic fungicide. If this disease becomes established you cannot grow any tulips in the same area for three years as the same problem will occur.

TULIP BREAKING VIRUS

This is spread by aphids and is therefore more of a problem for late-flowering varieties. Both leaves and flowers can become streaked. The virus can produce beautiful flowers but it will weaken the bulb and more significantly it will spread throughout your plants, including those of other species. Bite the bullet and lift and destroy both bulb and foliage. You can put the flower in a vase in the house.

Tulips as cut flowers

All tulip cultivars make wonderful cut flowers that are long-lasting and continue to grow even after they have been cut, sometimes as much as 6in (15cm). If you have the space for a cutting garden, plant bulbs in neat rows in autumn so that you can pick as you please in the spring; should you wish to plant a range of colors to mix together in arrangements, remember to select varieties that bloom at the same time. Alternatively, by choosing a selection of tulips that bloom from early to late spring you can enjoy them as cut flowers all through the spring.

Pick tulips at one day old, just as the petals just begin to open. Cut the stem by at least ½in (1cm), wrap in dry paper and stand in cold water for 6–8 hours somewhere cool before arranging. Keep them out of direct sunlight and remove any foliage that is below the water line as this will decompose. Always make sure your vase is clean before use and fill with cold water as tepid or warm water will make the stems liable to droop.

If you have purchased a bunch of tulips, cut the stem ends by at least ½in (1cm) to help water uptake and put them in a vase of water immediately. Change the water completely every two days to prevent harmful bacteria developing. Keep them out of strong sunlight and away from direct sources of heat such as radiators to prolong life. Tulips are phototropic, meaning that they bend towards the light, which creates wonderfully dynamic arrangements. Some people object to this and keep rotating the vase to keep the tulips upright, while others regard it as a charming character trait. If you want straight stems, when you cut the blooms wrap them firmly in a roll of damp newspaper and fasten this with rubber bands, then pop into water and leave overnight before arranging. With a bit of luck, they'll maintain a military bearing.

If you want to mix tulips and daffodils together in a vase you should first plunge the latter into a separate container for 4–8 hours as they emit sap that will harm the tulips if you combine them straight away. Use a fresh vase and fresh water for your arrangement.

If the need arises you can dry-store freshly cut flowers in tight bud out of water for up to a week in a refrigerator. When you are ready to use them, fill a bucket with water at 100–110°F (38–43°C). Cut 2in (5cm) from the bases of the stems and wrap the flowers in plastic so that the stems do not sit on the very bottom of the bucket, but a little above it, to enable water uptake. Leave them for two hours before using them in an arrangement. If you have a huge refrigerator you can wet-store tulips for a week in a bucket of water.

GLOSSARY

Anther The pollen-producing part of the plant, which rests atop the filament; together they make up the stamen.

Basal plate This is found at the base of the bulb, the immature plant stem grows from this inside the bulb, and the roots grow out of it.

Breaking The tulip breaking virus (or mosaic virus) is spread by aphids and causes a tulip to develop colorful flames in the petals. However, it weakens the bulb and its offsets, and ultimately kills it.

Bulb The bulb is a storage organ which nurtures and protects the developing plant. It also produces offsets, which in time will mature into bulbs.

Cultivar A cultivated variety that has been produced by selected breeding.

Deadheading Snipping off dead flowers from the plant. In tulips this ensures that the plant does not put any energy into producing seed, but instead the bulb utilizes nutrients to produce offsets.

Divisions There are 15 divisions of tulips which delineate the form as well as the type and time of flowering; see full details of each on pp.12–14.

Filament The leggy stem that supports the anther; together they make up the stamen.

Hybrid The crossing of different species or varieties.

Lifting When a tulip stem and leaves have withered back after flowering the bulbs are lifted from the soil so that the offsets can be removed.

Offset This is an immature bulb that can take one or more years to mature to flowering. A mother bulb can produce five offsets, which can be seen on lifting. One will be larger than the others and should, if stored correctly, be ready to flower the following year.

Pistil The term pistil incorporates the ovary, style and stigma of the tulip. The ovary, where fertilization takes place, is linked to the stigma, which receives the pollen that enables fertilization by the style.

Sport A change in the genetic make-up of a plant.

Stamen The flower's male reproductive parts, made up of the filament and the anther.

Stigma The tip of the pistil on which pollen is deposited to enable fertilization. The pollen travels from the stigma, down the style to fertilize the ovary, which goes on to form the seed pod.

Tepal Technically a tulip has neither sepals nor petals, but tepals. These are green when the flower is in bud but are imbued with color as the bud prepares to open. This makes it distinct from petals, which are imbued with color from the start, but protected by green sepals when the flower is in bud. For ease of reference the tepals have been described as petals throughout this book.

Tunic The thin papery outer coat of the bulb.

INDEX

DIRECTORY

This list covers the main entries that appear this book:

Other species tulips and varieties illustrated are as follows:

PUBLISHER'S ACKNOWLEDGMENTS

We are very grateful to all those who have helped with *Tulips*. Particular thanks goes to the following:

Joan Holmes for all her help sourcing, ordering and arranging the flowers for many of the photographs featured in this book, and for allowing us to use her lovely home as a location for our shoot.

Bloms Bulbs for supplying flowers for photography and to Elaine and Christopher Blom for casting an expert eye over photographs and copy.

Somang Lee for her wonderful illustrations.

Stef van Dam at Green Garden Flower Bulbs and Nathan Teeuw at Gee Tee Bulb Company for their help with planning the book.

AUTHOR'S ACKNOWLEDGMENTS

I must first pay tribute to the photographer Rachel Warne, whose superb eye has captured the whimsy, joy and overblown beauty of this magnificent flower. She has tramped the length and breadth of the country and crossed into Europe in her efforts to photograph perfect blooms and succeeded in tracking down the most elusive of varieties, without her this book would be nothing.

I have had assistance from more people than I can name, and without their patience and kindness in answering innumerable queries this book would not have come to fruition. In the Netherlands Stef van Dam of Green Garden Flower Bulbs gave helpful advice as to which bulb cultivars would be available for sale over the next few years. At the KAVB – the Royal General Bulb Growers' Association – Johan van Scheepen, taxonomist/librarian and Saskia Bodegom, taxonomist – have both provided invaluable research and information and I am in their debt. Jan de Wit, of Jan de Wit en Zonen B.V. was most helpful in filling the gaps in my knowledge and I am so grateful for his assistance. I must also thank Elaine and Christopher Blom of Bloms Bulbs for generously agreeing to share their expertise and check my copy.

At Pavilion I must thank my editors; the wonderful Krissy Mallett, kind Katie Hewett, and the patient and ever-vigilant Diana Vowles, for their gentle encouragement, forbearance, and enthusiasm. I must also salute Michelle Mac and Gail Jones for the elegant design, and Polly Powell and Katie Cowan for their faith in me.

I owe a debt of gratitude to my husband, Eric Musgrave, who sprang into action as deadlines loomed, whisking around with a duster and producing a diverting array of dishes from whatever was left in the fridge, a not inconsiderable challenge. Our lovely children Florence, Teddy and Genevieve and the fabulous Alexandra Huckstable were endlessly encouraging, and even tolerated my working through a family holiday after a move from Kent to Northumberland interrupted progress. Florence also kindly found time to proof read my first draft.

I must also acknowledge the kind encouragement of the Warehorne book group whose consternation in our monthly meetings that I was *still* writing about tulips spurred me on to finish. Ladies, I have missed you.

PHOTOGRAPHER'S ACKNOWLEDGMENTS

Making this beautiful book has been a wild and wonderful ride, and there never is enough room to thank everyone properly. First I would like to thank Pavilion for approaching me to step into the shoes of Georgianna Lane; I was so excited and very grateful to be asked. I can't thank you all enough, especially Krissy Mallet, commissioning editor and "my rock," for her countless emails, support and fantastic production – I love a spreadsheet! Thanks too to the rest of the team: Katie Cowan, Michelle Mac, Gail Jones, Diana Vowles and Katie Hewett. The stoic art director Helen Lewis, even with an injured foot on the styled shoot days, made them a breeze. I am also so grateful to Jane Eastoe, the wonderful writer, who brought this book to life; it's been an absolute joy working alongside you, thank you.

Thanks must also go to: Nathan at Gee Tee Bulb Company for his tireless help and kindness. Stef van Dam at Green Garden Flower Bulbs for going beyond the call of duty; I hope we will meet one day after all that! Martin Duncan, Flo Powell, Stephen Manion and Sandra Webber at Arundel Castle in West Sussex. I never need an excuse to visit Martin and his wife Georgina, they are so welcoming and generous. Martin's passion and expertise are wonderful to behold. Huge thanks to all at Arundel. Annemarie M.M. Gerards-Adriaansens at Keukenhof in Lisse, Netherlands, the epicenter of the tulip world, thank you for allowing me to shoot at your busiest time. Tom Brown, Head Gardener at Parham House and Gardens in West Sussex, your patience was greatly appreciated. Andy Boyton at Springfields Festival Gardens in Lincolnshire; in the face of extreme weather conditions this spring his tulips found a way due to his steadfast commitment to the tulip season. Florist Joan Holmes for her flair that makes even the naughtiest of tulips look a peach. My brother Stuart for his support and giving up his car in Holland! Lou Dedieu, my assistant, whose hard work and brains kept me sane, you will be missed. Richenda Whitehead and Paul Aston at Cambridge University Botanic Garden for keeping the species tulips going. Bloms Bulbs who supplied some of the flowers for the last shoot day. Kate Wilson at Pashley Manor Gardens in East Sussex – sorry we didn't make it. And of course, Joe for being Joe, and Erin my little poppet for being proud of her Mummy.

This book has taught me to never underestimate the power of nature. Climate change is real and it is making nature's time here all the more challenging. I hope this book will show the true beauty of tulips as they adjust and evolve in the face of adversity. Enjoy.

23 22 21 20 19   5 4 3 2

Published in the United States of America by
Gibbs Smith
PO Box 667
Layton, Utah 84041
1.800.835.4993 orders
www.gibbs-smith.com

Text copyright © 2019 Jane Eastoe
Photography copyright © 2019 Rachel Warne

ISBN 978-1-4236-5129-1
Library of Congress Control Number: 2018951233

First published in the United Kingdom in 2019 by
Pavilion
43 Great Ormond Street
London
WC1N 3HZ

Reproduction by Mission Productions, Ltd, Hong Kong
Printed in Singapore